Rails Across
the Prairies

Rails Across the Prairies

Ron Brown

The Railway Heritage of Canada's Prairie Provinces

DUNDURN
TORONTO

Editor: Matt Baker
Design: Jesse Hooper
Printer: Webcom

Library and Archives Canada Cataloguing in Publication

Brown, Ron, 1945-
　　Rails across the prairies : the railway heritage of Canada's prairie provinces / Ron Brown.

Includes index.
Issued also in electronic formats.
ISBN 978-1-4597-0215-8

　　1. Railroads--Prairie Provinces. 2. Railroads--Prairie Provinces--History. 3. Prairie Provinces--History. I. Title.

HE2809.P73B76 2012　　　385.09712　　　C2012-900133-3

1　2　3　4　5　　　16　15　14　13　12

We acknowledge the support of the **Canada Council for the Arts** and the **Ontario Arts Council** for our publishing program. We also acknowledge the financial support of the **Government of Canada** through the **Canada Book Fund** and **Livres Canada Books**, and the **Government of Ontario** through the **Ontario Book Publishing Tax Credit** and the **Ontario Media Development Corporation**.

Care has been taken to trace the ownership of copyright material used in this book. The author and the publisher welcome any information enabling them to rectify any references or credits in subsequent editions.

J. Kirk Howard, President

All photos by the author unless otherwise stated.

Printed and bound in Canada.
www.dundurn.com

Dundurn
3 Church Street, Suite 500
Toronto, Ontario, Canada
M5E 1M2

Gazelle Book Services Limited
White Cross Mills
High Town, Lancaster, England
LA1 4XS

Dundurn
2250 Military Road
Tonawanda, NY
U.S.A. 14150

Contents

Acknowledgements

How wonderful it was to travel across the Prairies and meet so many individuals and organizations who were concerned about their railway heritage. There were travel staff, hotel staff, museum curators, and simply those individuals who were passionate about their railway roots.

In no particular order, I would like to thank the curator of the station museum in Radville, Judy Dionne, who spent her valuable time showing me the wonderful work the local volunteers have done to preserve their station on site, and who forwarded to me some interesting old images of the station. Then there was Denis Depres of the Delta Bessborough Hotel in Saskatoon, who gave me the grand tour of a grand building, and Don McGuire, who led the creation of the Wainwright Rail Park, preserving much valuable rolling stack. Thanks to Barb Monroe, communications specialist at the Heritage Park Historical Village in Calgary, for providing much-needed images of their rail operations, and to Catriona Hill, director of the CPR's Heritage Services in Calgary, for also sharing some great shots of their heritage railway equipment, steam engine *2816*, and the glamorous *Royal Canadian Pacific* tour train. Michelle Grenier of Hudson Bay was also kind enough to send images of the heritage station in Al Mazur Memorial Heritage Park. Thanks, too, to Malcolm Andrew of VIA Rail Canada for the image of Edmonton's elegant and modern new VIA Rail station there. I am grateful to Andy and Michelle of the Rochfort Bridge Trading Post, who provided vital details of the massive railway trestle in that village, and Laurie Armstrong, director of economic development and tourism in Hanna, for updates on the relocation of the station and progress of the efforts to save that community's rare roundhouse.

Finally, I am most grateful to the friendly and helpful staff at Travel Alberta and Tourism Saskatchewan for generously assisting me with the logistics of my visits to those two provinces during the summer of 2011 (one of the wettest in years).

I hope this modest book will confirm to these people that their assistance has been worth it.

Introduction

There is no other part of our country that has been so utterly dependent upon the railway for its development than Canada's prairie provinces. Most of the towns and villages in eastern Canada were there long before the rails arrived, in some cases more than a century before. While the arrival of the railways may have helped shape the growth of these towns and villages, those in the Prairies owed their very existence to it.

The railways determined where the towns would go and how they would look. Railway planners laid out the streets and decided how each area would be used. Architects like R.B. Pratt, the Maxwell brothers, and Edward Colonna created stations that were often elegant — even grand — but in almost every case dominated the urban landscape. Railways were the lifeblood of nearly every town and village, with grain shipping forming the basis of the towns' economies. Divisional points established by the railways for their yards, engine maintenance, and crew layovers led to large towns, while major terminals created the prairie's largest cities.

Prairie residents who care about their local heritage must look to the railway and recognize, preserve, and celebrate its vestiges: the stations, the grain elevators, the water towers, the massive bridges, and the hotels. Regrettably, local indifference and even hostility to these reminders has trumped the efforts of those who cherish and attempt to save them.

This book is an attempt to bring attention to the few survivors of that heritage. Many bridges yet loom high about the wide prairie valleys; stations have been lovingly restored and converted to new uses, often museums. Grain elevators have become interpretive centres, and a handful of water towers yet remain; even a few of the many prairie ghost towns proudly proclaim their status. Railway museums have assembled large collections of the coaches and engines that brought the daily arrivals to the settlements. Steam excursions relive the sights and sounds and experiences of those historic times, although VIA Rail Canada remains the only living descendant of that legacy.

There are challenges, still. The demise of the Wheat Board threatens short lines, the few villages which yet depend upon their local grain elevators, and even the livelihoods of farmers themselves. Local attitudes may doom still more historic structures. Arson has cost the Prairies its most historic grain elevator, in Fleming, Saskatchewan, and a water tower in Glenborough, Manitoba. Yet, the desire to preserve and celebrate the history of a region that the railways largely created is growing. This book hopefully will be part of that celebration.

Chapter One

Rails Across the Prairies: The Rails Arrive

The Canadian Pacific Railway: Canada's National Dream

Having become the first prime minister of the newly created Dominion of Canada, the Tory John A. MacDonald worried about how to keep the country together. Concerns, real or not, about the Americans possibly wanting to annex Canada plagued him. The term *manifest destiny* had been uttered not too many years previous, and he worried, too, about the U.S. post-Civil War ambitions. And then there was the immense land mass between the settled east and the west coast that clearly had more ties to the south than to the east. In 1869 the first transcontinental railway in the U.S. had been completed, and the projected Northern Pacific route close to the border appeared poised to send branch lines northward into what were then the North West Territories. In order to entice the territory of British Columbia to join Confederation, and to secure the territories, in 1871 MacDonald promised a transcontinental railway.

Ground was broken in West Fort William in 1873, but a scandal brought down MacDonald's government, and it was not until his re-election that the railway building began, in 1881, when the Canadian Pacific Railway Company was formed.

Until the arrival of the railways, the most direct link of the Prairies to eastern Canada involved travel by steamer up the Red River to Saint Paul, Minnesota, where travellers could connect with the Union Pacific and Central Railway.

The first line into the Prairies, however, was not the CPR, but rather the Pembina Branch, built from Emerson on the Minnesota border to St. Boniface. It would later form part of the CPR. The route had been first proposed in 1874 by Prime Minister Alexander Mackenzie as an alternative to the scandal-plagued CPR backed by John A. MacDonald.

But, even before the line opened, the first steam engine arrived in Winnipeg. On October 9, 1877, the steamer *Selkirk* brought the Prairies' first steam locomotive, the *Countess of Dufferin*, to Point Douglas in Winnipeg. Its role was to help in the construction of the Pembina Branch, and today the steam engine rests in the Winnipeg Railway Museum in that city's Union Station.

In 1878 the last spike was driven to connect the Pembina Branch with the Saint Paul and Pacific Railroad at Rosseau River, Minnesota. This one-hundred-kilometre branch was shortly thereafter acquired by the CPR and used to help ship in supplies necessary for the westward push of its own rail line. In December 1879, a second locomotive arrived in Winnipeg, after crossing the ice-covered Red River. This was the *J.C. Haggart*, which would lead the construction westward from Winnipeg the following spring.

Now in the Winnipeg Rail Museum, the Countess of Dufferin *was the first steam locomotive to arrive on the prairies.*

Although the CPR was originally intended to lure the colony of British Columbia into the Canadian fold and speed settlement of the Prairies, it was also a convenient way to move the military quickly to potential trouble spots in the west. Despite the benefits to Canada, it was considered by its British backers to offer a vital link between Europe and Japan and was even nicknamed the "all red route."

After ground was broken in West Fort William (today Thunder Bay) in 1873 for the construction of the CPR, the citizens of Winnipeg realized, with concern, that the proposed route crossed the Red River well to their north, at Selkirk. Winnipeg quickly offered the CPR a generous grant of land and tax concessions if it would swing its line southward through Winnipeg. And so, in what would be a trend of accepting blatant inducements, the CPR agreed.

Because the CPR had too little capital to undertake the entire project, in 1881 the federal government passed the CPR Act, granting the railway twenty-five million dollars and twenty-five million acres of land, the sales of which would allow the CPR to raise the necessary funds. The railway then turned around and sold 2.2 million acres of that land to the Canadian North-West Land Company, with the right to buy five million more. The company proceeded to lay out townsites at intervals of twelve to fifteen kilometres — the distance that a farmer could haul a wagonload of grain in a day. Many of these sites are today's prairie ghost towns.

Although the CPR's original survey routed the line through the northern, more-fertile part of the Prairies, the railway opted instead to lay tracks farther south, partly in order to pre-empt incursions by American railroads.

Construction proceeded swiftly across the open prairies. At the end of rail, the work train included a pair of two-storey cars for the crew; an upper level was for sleeping, the lower for eating. Twenty flat cars held the ties and rails while inspection cars and workshops completed the consist. After the tracklayers came the station builders. The first crew erected the framing, the next did the sheeting and flooring, while the final crew finished off the plastering and painting.

It was not unusual for four or five stations to be under way at the same time. It was no surprise, then, that by 1881, trains were entering Brandon, and just two years later, Calgary. Finally, on November 1, 1885, the Prairies were linked to eastern Canada and train service between Montreal and Winnipeg began.

To further discourage American incursions, the CPR then constructed a line of its own into the U.S., namely the "Soo" line, which stretched from a point near Moose Jaw to the U.S. border at North Portal, where it linked with routes to Chicago.

Following the opening of the CPR to Port Moody and then Vancouver in 1886, rail construction in the Prairies, except for a few branch lines, slowed to a crawl. The CPR at that time suffered no real competition, creating a monopoly that left farmers paying high prices to move their wheat. Pressure mounted on Manitoba's premier, Norquay, to provide competition by chartering new provincial railways. The MacDonald government, however, still very much in league with the CPR, disallowed any such initiative. George Stephen, president of the CPR, went even further and threatened to move the CPR shops from Winnipeg to Fort William. In response the provincial attorney threatened to subpoena Stephen along with Donald Smith, but, hidden in a CPR coach, they slipped out of the province before he could do so.

After an economic depression slowed railway construction in the early 1890s, the CPR returned to branch-line building and by 1897 had managed to lay another 3,500 kilometres of track, nearly half of it on branch lines. The province of Manitoba added another eight hundred kilometres of provincially chartered short lines. These included the Manitoba and Northwestern from Portage la Prairie to Yorkton (in what would become Saskatchewan), and the Northern Pacific and Manitoba Railway from Emerson to Winnipeg and from Morris to Brandon. Although the Lake Manitoba Railway and Canal had been chartered to build from Gladstone to Sifton as early as 1889, it remained for the Canadian Northern Railway to assume control of the charter to begin construction. Within twenty years, Manitoba had tripled its trackage.

While rail lines were criss-crossing the Manitoba landscape prior to 1900, the western prairies had little to show. Although the CPR had laid tracks into Calgary by 1883, it was not until 1891 that it extended branches north to Strathcona, under the charter of the Calgary and Edmonton Railway (C&E), and south to Fort Macleod.

In 1891 the C&E arrived in South Edmonton (soon to be called Strathcona) from Calgary but remained on the south bank of the North Saskatchewan River, much to the chagrin of Edmontonians who were waiting on the north bank. But it was here that it laid out yards and built a modest wooden station. The C&E was, in reality, part of the CPR, which later built a more elaborate stone-and-brick station, still standing in historic Strathcona. It was not until 1913 that the CPR finally crossed the then-new High Level Bridge and entered Edmonton.

In 1889 the CPR extended a branch line from its main line near Medicine Hat to the coal fields near Lethbridge. Until then, the North Western Coal and Navigation Company had been barging coal from Lethbridge to the CPR at Medicine Hat, but the shallow water forced it to build a line of its own. In 1889 the CPR extended the Lethbridge line down to the American border at Coutts to link with the American railway network.

The only other line of note on the western prairies at this time was the Qu'Appelle Long Lake and Saskatchewan Railway (QLL&S), built in 1889–90 from Regina to the steamer landing on the North Saskatchewan River at Prince Albert. Although effectively owned by the CPR, it was built under a separate charter so that the QLL&S could obtain the land grants in that area. The contractors who built that line were none other than William Mackenzie and Donald Mann. Little could the CPR know that they would soon launch the line's main railway rival — the Canadian Northern Railway.

The Canadian Northern Railway Empire of William Mackenzie and Donald Mann

Once they were finished with the QLL&S, Mackenzie and Mann began to create their own empire, which they called the Canadian Northern Railway. Together, their policy was to establish a national network by buying up unprofitable lines and unused charters, building lines as quickly and cheaply as possible to access as many areas as they could. Mann had previously acquired the charter for the Hudson Bay Railway, and as partners, he and Mackenzie began by acquiring the charters of the Winnipeg Great Northern Railway and the Lake Manitoba Railway and Canal Company, both of which would be the beginnings of a main line that would stay to the north of the CPR. Completed in 1905, the route extended through Dauphin and North Battleford, where it kept north of the North Saskatchewan River, and then continued on to Edmonton.

Political pressure from Prince Albert would also lead to a second "main line" to that area. Although Mackenzie and Mann's tracks reached Prince Albert from Dauphin in 1906, another decade would pass before the line from Prince Albert would join up with their first main line east of North Battleford. From North Battleford, Mackenzie and Mann had intended to build yet another line north and west to open the area north of the North Saskatchewan — an area which was already attracting large numbers of Ukrainian settlers. Construction began from North Battleford at one end and from Edmonton at the other, but the lines were still unconnected when the CNo went broke. It remained for the CNR to take over construction, although even it failed to complete the link.

During this time, the CNo concentrated on establishing a dense network of branch lines to reach as many farmers as possible. Always interested in encouraging more competition for the hated CPR, the Manitoba government leased more than 450 kilometres of track from the Northern Pacific and conveyed it to the two railway builders. Meanwhile, Robert Montgomery Horne-Payne, founder of the British Empire Trust Company, was raising money for Canadian ventures, and he awarded two hundred million dollars to Mackenzie and Mann. They promptly put it toward assembling another eight hundred kilometres of new line, much of it intruding into CPR territory. They then took over a pair of charters that allowed them to connect with Port Arthur via Minnesota. In 1908 they began work on another vital link, taking them from Saskatoon to Calgary by way of Drumheller, a route that they didn't complete until 1914. In 1912 the CNo added yet another line to its empire by extending a resource route north from Edmonton to the Athabasca River.

By 1915, when the two empire builders had driven the last spike at Kamloops Junction, the CNo had laid more than fifteen thousand kilometres of track and created 550 new communities.

Despite this impressive feat, the financial woes that would ultimately defeat them were showing as early as 1907, when they failed to make sufficient earnings to cover their interest charges. Efforts to sell some branches to the provinces found no takers. Instead, they incorporated many of their proposed new branch lines under provincial charters, avoiding the need for federal approval. One such example was the Alberta Midland Railway (AMR), which the Alberta legislature chartered in February of 1909. The lines AMR completed were from Vegreville to Calgary and from Camrose to South Edmonton (later Strathcona), before becoming part of the CNo system.

But the CNo's fortunes rebounded, and two years later it had extended tracks all the way to the Atlantic. However, the election of Robert Borden as prime minister in 1911 proved to be another financial setback, and the CNo sought help first from England and then the U.S. With the war then raging, Britain could no longer export capital — a similar dilemma to the one facing Americans after belatedly entering the war in 1917. In that year, the end effectively came for Mackenzie and Mann's railway empire, when a royal commission recommended that the government assume control of the line.

The Edmonton, Yukon and Pacific Railway

Originally chartered in 1896 as the Edmonton District Railway, this line was intended to stretch to the gold fields of the Yukon. By 1898, however, no work had been done and the charter fell into the ambitious hands of Mackenzie and Mann and their growing Canadian Northern Railway Empire. They changed the name to the Edmonton, Yukon and Pacific (EY&P), whose charter allowed a route to the Pacific. Under the EY&P, the CNo finally linked Edmonton and Strathcona by constructing its line along the Mill Creek Ravine and crossing the North Saskatchewan River on the "Low Level Bridge," which the federal government had built in 1900. In 1902 the CNo entered Edmonton, building its station below McDougall Hill. Meanwhile, the main line of the CNo arrived in Edmonton from the east in 1905, and the company built a station on 21st Street. An EY&P trestle still survives on the hiking trail that follows the rail right-of-way through the Mill Creek Ravine.

The Alberta Midland Railway

Chartered in 1909, this line runs from Vegreville to Calgary, with a short-lived "short cut" from Camrose to Edmonton. It was really an instrument of the Canadian Northern Railway, using a provincial charter to get around federal approval for its construction. In fact, once the charter was approved by Alberta, it immediately became part of the CNo. Its route took it through the coal fields of the Drumheller badlands, past the ghost town of Wayne, and along the valley of the Rosebud River and Serviceberry Creek, where sixty-two bridges were needed.

Laurier's National Dream: The Grand Trunk Pacific Railway, Canada's Third Transcontinental Line

Despite the building of the CPR and the CNo, prairie settlement still lagged, and the new Liberal government of Wilfrid Laurier tasked Interior Minister Clifford Sifton to encourage more immigration, largely from Britain and eastern Europe. By 1911, seven hundred thousand immigrants had been persuaded and arrived seeking the "Last Best West," as the brochures proclaimed. It helped that, in 1905, Charles Sounder, the Dominion "cerealist," developed a type of wheat known as Marquis wheat, which could grow in harsher climates and less-fertile soil.

Meanwhile, the Grand Trunk Railway (GTR), which dominated eastern Canada, had been casting its own eyes toward the transcontinental cash cow since 1856 and lobbied to be let in. The Laurier government agreed and granted a charter to the Grand Trunk Pacific for a national line. But the GTR was hesitant to expend the large sums needed to build a line through the harsh terrain of northern Ontario and Quebec. Indeed, with the need for a third national railway being constantly questioned, the GTR sought to instead obtain the CNo. Mackenzie and Mann, however, refused to part with their own national dream.

Finally, Laurier agreed to the third national railway. To help the GTR financially, Laurier agreed that the eastern portion of the new railway would be built by the government itself and would become known as the National Transcontinental Railway (NTR), while the western portion from Winnipeg to Prince Rupert would be the responsibility of the GTR and would be known as the Grand Trunk Pacific (GTP). The two lines would meet in Winnipeg.

But, unlike the CNo, the GTP had little interest in branch lines and instead aimed straight for the coast, ultimately reaching Prince Rupert in 1914. From Winnipeg the GTP's alignment took it through Melville, Saskatoon, and Edmonton, although it did add branch lines to Prince Albert and through Regina to the American border.

In building the eastern portion, the National Transcontinental Railway conquered countless construction hurdles, and structural engineers consider the construction of that line the world's greatest feat of engineering in the early twentieth century outside of the Panama Canal. Conversely, the Grand Trunk Pacific's western segment was relatively straightforward: in 1905 the GTP turned sod in Carberry, Manitoba, and in just two years, the heavy-duty steel rails were being pounded into Saskatoon. By 1910 they were in Edmonton.

Because of the heavier steel rail, the GTP trains could haul longer and heavier loads than could the CNo, and passenger trains between Winnipeg and Edmonton beat their rivals by four hours. West of Edmonton, and into the mountains near Jasper, the CNo and GTP tracks ran parallel to each other. Finally, common sense prevailed, and in 1917 the CNo switched to the heavier GTP track, while the redundant CNo rails were sent to wartime France to replace tracks damaged by bombing.

But, unlike the CPR and the CNo, the GTP received no grants of land. Instead, it went ahead and purchased forty-five thousand acres of land for eighty-six townsites, advertising them as "towns made to order."

As early as 1911, it was becoming painfully clear that too much track had been laid in western Canada. With costs soaring, Charles Melville Hays, president of the GTP, urged the government to take control of the line, but that initiative sank in 1912, when Hays went down with the *Titanic*. In fact, the government itself was urging the GTP to take over the NTR and CNo, but to no avail. Between 1900 and 1915, trackage increased by 130 percent, whereas population increased by only 40 percent. Compared to the U.S. and the U.K., Canada's lines were the most sparsely populated, at 1.5 kilometres of track for every 250 people — a far cry from the 1.5 kilometres per four hundred people in the U.S., and 1.5 kilometres per two thousand in the U.K. Even the influential Bank of Commerce, which owned banks in many prairie towns, was calling for a national railway system for the country.

Eventually, outright fraud and shady practices had increased the cost of operating the NTR section to the point where the GTR refused to continue operating it. The need to fund the war effort meant that the many lines in the Prairies suffered in a similar fashion to route right across the country. In 1916 Prime Minister Robert Borden established a royal commission, which urged that the federal government amalgamate the GTR, GTP, CNo, NTR, and ICR. The federal government ignored a CPR plea to assimilate the lines with its own and instead created the Canadian Government Railways to operate the eastern division of the GTR as well as the failing Intercolonial Railway. In 1918 the Canadian National Railway was created to take over the operations of both the Canadian Northern and the Grand Trunk Pacific Railways. Later, in 1919, the government passed the Grand Trunk Acquisition Act and the following year had control of both the GTP and GTR. The Canadian National Railway was formally born. But would it save the Prairie rail lines?

The Canadian National Railway

Under its new president, Henry W. Thornton, the Canadian National Railway could embark on new railway ventures, including restarting the moribund Hudson Bay Railway. Through the 1920s, the new CNR added branch lines and station styles of its own. It also merged the two CPR-operated lines to the Peace District. One of the CNR's tasks at hand was to complete unfinished lines it had inherited, such as a branch the CNo had, in 1911, promised to build in order to open up the area north of the North Saskatchewan River between Edmonton and North Battleford. Under a province of Alberta charter for the "Canadian Northern Western Railway," the CNo surveyed a northerly route from Edmonton to Saskatchewan to meet a section that had already been completed north of North Battleford to St. Walburg.

Progress on the western end had remained slow from the beginning, halting altogether with the onset of the First World War. With the return of more prosperous times in the 1920s, the CNR — now the new owner of the CNo — began work anew. While rails were extended to Grande Centre and Heinsburg, the final link to St. Walburg in Saskatchewan remained unrealized. Abandoned in the late 1990s, that portion of the old route between Waskatenau, Heinsburg, and Cold Lake later became the route of the popular Iron Horse Trail.

But the CNR fared little better than its predecessors, as traffic fell by half between 1928 and 1935. In fact, to keep up with changing transportation realities, the CNR began using trucks and joined the CPR in launching Canadian Airways Ltd. in 1930. Following the Second World War, the auto age took hold and rail traffic dwindled. To keep profitable, the CNR and CPR began to eliminate tracks and reduce service. Today, the trimmer lines still operate expansive yards and haul lengthy unit trains across the vast plains. Ironically, many of their so-called uneconomical branch lines have become profitable short lines that still link dozens of small prairie towns and the farmers who depend on them.

The Churchill train pauses at Portage la Prairie station in Manitoba.

The Hudson Bay Railway

Interest in a railway to the shores of Hudson's Bay dates back to the early 1880s, when charters were granted to two separate companies: the Nelson Valley Railway and Transportation Company and the Winnipeg and Hudson Bay Railway and Steamship Company, which eventually merged to form the Winnipeg Great Northern Railway, later renamed the Manitoba Railway and Canal Company. This was the very charter that William Mackenzie and Donald Mann used to form the beginnings of their Canadian Northern Railway. In 1905, when the Canadian Northern Railway assumed the charter, it completed the Hudson Bay line to Hudson Bay Junction and then as far north as the Saskatchewan River at The Pas. However, it was more interested in using the charter to complete its main line to Edmonton, and it declined to carry the line farther north to the proposed terminal at Port Nelson without more funding from the government — funding that was not forthcoming.

In 1913 an exasperated federal government assumed the route, completing a bridge over the Saskatchewan River and laying track to Gillam, as well as starting work on the port facilities at Port Nelson. After being interrupted by the war, the Canadian National Railway took over and finished the line to Churchill rather than the inferior Port Nelson. In 1929 the trains started running over the eight-hundred kilometre line. Although grain shipments from this area were disappointing due to the short ice-free season, large mineral finds in the Thompson and Lynn Lake areas brought more business to the line. With prospects of global warming bringing longer ice-free seasons in the Arctic, interest in grain shipping has gained new life. As well, one of VIA Rail's more popular rail excursions is the Churchill train, which also serves remote aboriginal communities along the way.[1]

The Northern Pacific and Manitoba Railway

By 1888 many prairie farmers and residents in general resented the CPR monopoly and clamoured for competition, but the federal government was in no mood to charter another rail-building fiasco. The provincial government in Manitoba, however, was anxious to satisfy its own constituents and had no such hesitation. It happily granted approval to the Northern Pacific and Manitoba (NP&M) to build a line south from Winnipeg to the U.S. border at Emerson, and west to Brandon.

By travelling south, passengers could transfer to the Northern Pacific Railway and voyage to the west coast, all in competition with the CPR. In Winnipeg the NP&M chose the forks of the Assiniboine and Red Rivers to build its station, engine house, and roundhouse. By 1901, however, financial woes befell the little line and it was taken over by the ambitious rail builders William McKenzie and Donald Mann, who were then cobbling together their Canadian Northern Railway network.

When the GTP and CNo built its magnificent Union Station in Winnipeg in 1911, the former NP&M station became an immigration hall. Later redesigned, the old NP&M engine house then became the Bridges and Structures Building. With the development of the Forks, it was transformed into the Manitoba Children's Museum and forms part of the revitalization project. Adjacent to today's children's museum, the Johnson Terminal is the new home of what were once the GTP and the NP&M stables.

The Northern Alberta Railway

As the Peace River area began interest farmers, a rail line was needed into that northwestern area. When the Edmonton, Dunvegan and British Columbia Railway (ED&BC) was chartered in 1907, it was intended to go through Dunvegan and trace the various river valleys to Fort George, British Columbia. But, instead of reaching Dunvegan, it went as far as Spirit River and then branched off to Grande Prairie, and from there it pushed through to Dawson Creek. Shortly after the province chartered the ED&BC line, it also chartered the Alberta and Great Waterways Railway to build to the forks of the Clearwater and Athabasca Rivers — a route that was eventually completed by the ED&BC. In 1925 the town of Waterways was laid out. Today, it's a suburb of Fort McMurray.

Then, in 1913, the Alberta government chartered yet a third line, the Canada Central line, to build from near

A former rail car sits in front of the GWWD station in St. Boniface, Manitoba.

McLennan to Peace River Crossing. The three lines then worked together until financial constraints forced the government to take over all three. In 1928 the lines were taken over by the CPR and CNR, who called line the Northern Alberta Railway. In 1981 that line was assumed solely by the CNR.

In 1962 the Canadian government began constructing the Great Slave Lake Railway from Roma to Hay River on Great Slave Lake — a distance of some 520 kilometres. The Alberta Resources Railway was completed by the Alberta Government in 1969 and runs for thirty-two kilometres, from Hinton to Grande Prairie.

The Greater Winnipeg Water District Railway

The Greater Winnipeg Water District Railway (GWWD) enjoys a long and significant history in the annals of Manitoba railways. To supply water to the booming city of Winnipeg, the Government of Manitoba proposed to build an aqueduct to the parched city from Shoal Lake near the Ontario border. The GWWD railway was built in 1919 to service the aqueduct, and it still does. The 180-kilometre-long railway carried passengers — settlers in the early years and cottagers later on — and a wide range of freight including mail, milk, sand and gravel, and farm produce.

There were a small number of stations along the way, with names like Braintree, Waugh, Haddashville, and Millbrook, some of which survive in different locations. Now owned by the City of Winnipeg, the GWWD is considered to be the world's longest industrial rail line, operating three diesels for the sole purpose of maintaining the aqueduct.

The "Rimby Line"

Occasionally, farmers had to take things into their own hands. When no railway seemed prepared to extend tracks north from Lacombe, Alberta, to Rimby, the local farmers started one of their own. Although they obtained their charter in 1909, construction did not begin until 1913, and it took another eight years, due to the intervening war, to reach Rimby. In 1922 the CPR took over the line and completed a loop through Breton, eventually reaching Leduc in 1931. There is a CPR portable station — originally located in Tees — in the Paskapoo heritage village in Rimby, and this represents the type of station that would have stood in the town. A caboose stands beside it.

Watering the West

In 1903 the Government of Canada transferred over the last of the land it had promised to the CPR. The difficulty was that much of the 1.2 million hectares lay within what early surveyor John Palliser called nothing more than an extension of the American desert, noting that it was a "region of arid plains devoid of timber or pasturage of good quality." The region became known as the "Palliser Triangle."

West of Calgary, the prospects seemed equally dim. Here, in 1905, the CPR created a 2.5-square-kilometre reservoir — known as Chestermere lake — on the Bow River and in 1910 established a system of secondary canals. In 1944 the area was transferred to a local farmers' organization known as the Western Irrigation District, but the bigger challenge still lay to the east, in the Palliser Triangle.

The prospects of attracting settlement to what many perceived as a parched wasteland seemed dim, but the CPR saw potential and in 1910 launched an ambitious project to bring water to this arid prairie. At Bassano the railway constructed a massive dam and aqueduct, while south of Brooks it created Alberta's largest man-made lake: Lake Newell, five kilometres wide and sixteen kilometres long. These projects brought water to 113,000 hectares of cropland, luring a fresh influx of farm settlers.

THE UNUSUAL BROOKS AQUEDUCT

East of the bustling town of Brooks, Alberta, and a few kilometres south of the busy Trans-Canada Highway, stretches one the Prairies' most unusual railway structures — the Brooks Aqueduct.

Completed in 1914, the aqueduct extended more than three kilometres from the Bassano dam, and at the time it was the largest concrete structure in the world. In all, more than three hundred labourers poured nineteen thousand cubic metres of reinforced concrete, and they even included a siphon, which carried the water under the CPR line and back up again. In operation the aqueduct could move seventy cubic metres of water per second along the 3.2-kilometre system.

Within three years, pieces of concrete were falling off. To remedy this, a material known as gunnite was added, and by 1934 rehabilitation of the aqueduct was complete. But by then, the effects of the depression were hampering the CPR's ability to continue to operate the aqueduct, and a farmer's cooperative was formed to operate the valuable watering system. It had, after all, turned one of the driest parts of Alberta into one of its most fertile. In 1969 the federal and provincial governments assumed operations of the Eastern Irrigation District, and upon discovering that the aqueduct was quickly deteriorating,

they decided to demolish it. But the new management board for the district recognizing the heritage value of this rare structure and lobbied to retain it, fencing if off to protect the public.

The Brooks Aqueduct forms an unusual image on the landscape but was vital to irrigation in this dry corner of the prairies.

Until 1979 the aqueduct had irrigated the vast area, but finally the water trickled to a halt. Just four years later, it was declared a National Historic Site, and today it is an interpretive centre with early photographs to show this remarkable feat of construction to astonished visitors. A pathway follows the remaining portion of the aqueduct to the west, while to the east the CPR now passes through a gap in the structure.

THE BASSANO DAM

Equally impressive, however, is the Bassano dam, constructed to provide the water for the aqueduct. Located eight kilometres southwest of the town of Bassano, the 2,100-metre long earthen dam required 567,000 cubic metres of earth to build it. The concrete centre portion is 220 metres long. The dam was refurbished in 1984, and today is almost as popular an attraction as the aqueduct itself. The site offers a viewing point and picnic facilities.

Chapter Two

The Towns

Nearly every town, city, and village across the Prairies — including the numerous ghost towns — owe their heritage to the railways that created them. As part of the government's incentive package for the CPR, the railway received twenty-five million acres of free land. The tract consisted of every odd-numbered section to a depth of thirty-six kilometres from its route. In turn, the CPR sold more than two million acres to the affiliated Canada Northwest Land Company to create townsites along the line.

While the CNo was granted land for townsites, the Grand Trunk Pacific received no land grants and was obliged to acquire land for its eighty-six towns.

After the sites had been chosen, the next step was to attract buyers, not just to the towns, but to the farmland as well. With most potential settlers using the Canadian West as little more than a channel to the U.S., both the CPR and the Canadian government went into high gear to attract settlement. Interior Minister Clifford Sifton targeted the British in particular but also eastern Europeans, believing these "men in the sheepskin coats" were best-suited to adapt to the harsh prairie winters. Some of these groups included Icelanders, who were given their own "Republic of Iceland" in Manitoba; Scandinavians; and Russian Jews, who were allowed to create their own centralized settlements located away from their farmland.

The CPR had attracted 185 Hungarian families to the Qu'Appelle Valley as early as 1885. By the turn of the century, the CPR was using posters, excursions with editors, colonization companies, and, later on, even film promotions. Its booklet, *The Last Best West*, may not have been a "best-seller," but it drew the immigrants.

By 1920 the West had welcomed two million new settlers — a dramatic rise from the 400,000 in 1901. But not all were welcome. Non-whites were turned away through such devices as the Chinese head tax, agreements with foreign governments (Japan), the continuous journey requirement (south Asians), and medical "exams" (African-Americans).[2]

Townsite locations had little to do with geography and more to do with the simple economics of moving grain. During the days of horse-drawn grain wagons and wretched roads (even then), the distance that the horses could endure was about twelve to fifteen kilometres. And so that is how the railways located their towns. The grain companies would erect their elevators at these intervals, and here, too, the railways located their stations, around which they laid out the towns. While all townsites required at least a seven-hundred-metre passing track, alternate towns also included a water tower, section house, and a 350-metre business siding.

Townsites were usually identical, with a grid network of streets. If the main street did not run directly back from the station, it sometimes ran parallel to the tracks. A standard plan devised by Sandford Fleming depicted a grid, but one in which the streets were laid out diagonally to the tracks. Towns like Indian Head and North Battleford, both in Saskatchewan, adopted this layout.

The railways also specifically dictated how the towns would develop. Streets were to be twenty metres wide, with no space specifically allocated for businesses worth less than $1,000. In fact, the railways always ensured that the prime locations went to banks and hotels. The bank buildings were often prefabricated in British Columbia and shipped in pieces to be reassembled on the main street. Even the street names were often dictated by the railways, with sometimes imaginative results (mentioned later in the section on names).

Railways had the ability to dictate the land-use pattern, especially in large cities. Such tactics as donating parcels of

Although the historic station is now boarded up, the tracks in Humboldt, Saskatchewan, remain in use as a divisional point

land for hospitals, police stations, and town halls, and the laying out of upscale residential areas such as Mount Royal and Sunalta in Calgary, all helped direct the urban shape. The Grand Trunk Pacific went even further and introduced a crude form of zoning in its townsites.

Often, the railways provided the only parks in the little villages, in the form of station gardens. To challenge the notion that the Prairies were little more than desert, the railway companies established nurseries that provided plants and shrubs to the station agents. Some the more impressive gardens in the Prairies were to be found in places like Moose Jaw and Medicine Hat.

Because the steam engines could only travel 150 kilometres before refuelling, larger towns known as divisional points were established at these intervals. Such centres enjoyed larger or more decorative stations, bunkhouses for the train crews, roundhouses, and coal docks. Where two or more rail lines converged, the town grew even larger — places like Regina, Winnipeg, Saskatoon, Moose Jaw, Medicine Hat, Yorkton, Melville, Prince Albert, and Edmonton, all of which developed into important rail hubs.

The peak period of the smaller prairie towns was between 1920 and 1930. During this time, the CNR had assumed control of the bankrupt CNo and GTP and began to add more branch lines. To compete the CPR had to follow suit, but with the Depression and a long period of drought, village growth stagnated, and once-bustling communities began to wither.

Following the Second World War, cars and trucks began to replace rail travel. Steam locomotives were shunted into scrap yards as the railways rolled out their new diesel engines. This meant that trains could be longer, and there would be fewer of them. Diesels could travel farther with less fuel and, importantly, no water. This eliminated many of the railway functions that the towns and villages depended on, such as water towers, coal docks, and even stations themselves. With greater distances between divisional stops, every other divisional town lost those functions. Roundhouses and bunkhouses were demolished, workforces reduced.

Where tracks still exist, a number of former divisional points have retained a small workforce of railway workers. Places like Humboldt, Wilkie, Bredenbury, Medicine Hat, Wynyard, Biggar, and Melville, as well as dozens more, remain busy railway communities and have even constructed new facilities for their workforces. In other communities, such as Kerrobert, only a few sidings remain and the station sits vacant. Lanigan, Big Valley, Hanna, and Wainwright are examples of one-time divisional points where sidings have been lifted and stations closed.

In the face of truck competition, and centralization of grain elevators, many branch lines proved uneconomical and were abandoned. Stations and elevators vanished by the hundreds.

This was more than many of the little trackside towns could bear, and many shrivelled into ghost towns. Businesses were shuttered, children bussed to distant schools, and jobs fled to the cities — a situation the federal government is exacerbating by ending the Canada Wheat Board.

The Names

It seems that many of the railway companies rather enjoyed the prospect of naming the stations and the towns that they created. The Grand Trunk Pacific is well-known for alphabetizing its station names, and it managed to get through the alphabet three times in the Prairies and at least once in Ontario. The names between Winnipeg and Prince Rupert included Atwater to Zelma, Allan to Zumbro, and Bloom to Zenata.

While the Canadian Northern preferred to name its towns after its own employees and executives, it did venture into the literary world by naming the townsites between Bienfait and Maryfield, in southeastern Saskatchewan, after poets such as Lampman Browning, Wordsworth, Carlyle, Cowper, Service, Parkman, Mair, and Ryerson. After naming the town of Mozart after the great composer, the CPR set about naming streets after Liszt, Schubert, Haydn, and Wagner, among others. Loyalty to the crown also figured prominently in the CPR's "Empress" line, with Monarch, Empress, Duchess, and Princess. Consort, Throne, Coronation, Sovereign, Veteran, and Loyal were all so-named on a line built by the CPR in 1911 to celebrate the coronation of King George V. A military-fealty theme came with Major, Ensign, Forward, Federal, and Hussar — again, all CPR towns.

Sometimes, the railways would blend provincial and even state names, coming up with such combinations as Alsask, Altario, Mankota, and Mantario.

The most common names, however, were reserved for railway employees or executives. In 1908 a special GTP train made its way across the new line, with three executives on board: Charles Melville Hayes, William Wainwright, and William Hodgins Biggar. They were seeking locations for the line's divisional points, and it came as little surprise that those locations should bear the names Melville, Biggar, and Wainwright. The divisional point of Rivers in Manitoba was named to honour Sir Charles Rivers Wilson, chairman of the GTP's board of directors. In at least one case, the CPR chose to spell an employee's name backwards, Retlaw (Walter). Near Drumheller, the CPR reversed the letters of its Rosedale Junction station, calling it Eladesor Jc.

The Canadian Northern Railway, though, was the only railway to actually name a town after itself. Canora uses the first two letters from each of the railway's three names: Ca-No-Ra.

Body parts also served as inspiration, with Elbow and Eyebrow in Saskatchewan (although Elbow referred to a bend in the river) and even the delightfully named Owlseye in Alberta and Birdtail in Manitoba. International diplomacy received its due consideration in Togo, Saskatchewan, named after the Japanese Admiral Heihachiro Togo, who defeated the Russian fleet at the battle of Tsushima during the Russian-Japanese war of 1904–05 (the name was chosen because of Britain's support of Japan). The town of Mikado was also named in support of Japan. Russia, meanwhile, earned its share of recognition with the name Makaroff, after the vice-admiral of the Imperial Russian Navy during the same conflict.

Perhaps the two most intriguing communities, with regard to their names, are Moose Jaw and Medicine Hat. The latter likely derives from longer "Medicine Man's Hat." Oral tradition suggests that, during a battle between Cree and Blackfoot tribes, a Cree medicine man dropped his hat in the South Saskatchewan River. Taking this as a bad omen, the Cree fled the battlefield. When the Blackfoot found the hat, in celebration they named the location Medicine Hat Crossing. When the CPR arrived in 1883, it simply adopted the English translation of the local name for its station.

As early as 1857, surveyor John Palliser marked the name "Moose Jaw Bone Creek" on his map of the dry southern prairies. This likely referred either to the shape of the river at this point or that a moose's jaw was found here. Records don't indicate which. Again, the CPR used this existing local name when it established a divisional point here.

Cities

The concentration of railway activities turned some towns into the Prairies' major metropolises. These included Winnipeg, Regina, Edmonton, Saskatoon, and Calgary, often at the expense of towns with earlier promise, like Fort Macleod, Battleford, and Emerson. Major regional centres developed at Moose Jaw, Medicine Hat, Brandon, Lethbridge, Prince Albert, Red Deer, Estevan, Yorkton, and Dauphin.

WINNIPEG

The forks of the Red River and the Assiniboine River had been a focal point for settlement long before the trains arrived, and indeed even before European settlers crept in. The first, of course, were the settlers of Lord Selkirk's Red River colony, who arrived in 1813 at Douglas Point (the 5th Earl of Selkirk, Lord Selkirk's actual name was Thomas Douglas.) At around the same time, across the river in 1818, in what is today Saint Boniface, Father Joseph Norbert Provencher was creating a Roman Catholic mission.

Steamers plied the waters of the two rivers connecting the Red River colony and the mission. Travel to eastern Canada required a journey by steamer or stage to a railhead, then taking a train through the U.S.

Railways first reached the region in 1879, when the Pembina Branch laid its tracks from Winnipeg into Grand Rapids Minnesota, upstream on the Red River. Clearly, the newly created government of the Dominion of Canada believed that an all-Canadian route was in the country's best interests.

Following its groundbreaking in West Fort William in 1875, the CPR remained effectively stalled until the government of John A. MacDonald, the line's main supporter, was re-elected. Eventually, in 1883, the first CPR trains began operating in Winnipeg. At first, the CPR had proposed to bridge the Red River farther downstream, at North Kildonan, but when the Winnipeg city council offered the railway company free land and tax relief, the CPR altered the route to pass through Winnipeg. Nearly 20 years would pass before the Canadian Northern and the Grand Trunk Pacific railways joined forces to build one of the Prairies' grandest urban stations and lay out their yards and shops at the Forks. As it was also the home of the wheat exchange, and the capital of the new province of Manitoba, Winnipeg quickly evolved into western Canada's "Chicago."

Although the railways play a lesser role today in the city's fortunes, both the CNR and the CPR maintain major marshalling yards in the city. Both companies' grand urban stations have survived, as has the CNR hotel, the Fort Garry, although the CPR's Royal Alexandra Hotel has not. While the CNR has moved its yards from the location, many of the early railway buildings have been converted into markets and museums, with walkways following the rail beds and bridges. Now known as the Forks, this area constitutes a popular attraction for tourists and locals alike.

Saint Boniface developed around the church and mission, as railways played a small role in the community. The Greater Winnipeg Water District Railway did, however, place its terminal here — a fine stone building that yet serves as the headquarters for that single-purpose railway.

TRANSCONA

Transcona was one of those rare communities that depended entirely upon the railway for its economy. When Canada's prime minister, Wilfrid Laurier at the time, decided that Canada needed yet a third major rail line across the country, a joint construction effort began. The government-owned National Transcontinental would handle the eastern portion, and the Grand Trunk affiliate, the Grand Trunk Pacific, would be responsible for the western portion. The two routes met midway at Transcona, east of Winnipeg.

Construction on Transcona and its facilities began in 1908 and was finished by 1912. By 1916 it had become Manitoba's second-largest town; massive yards and important maintenance facilities provided work for the entire town.

Pandora and Bond Streets mark the centre of the town, where the gates to the historic "Midway" allow workers in and out of the vast network of shops. Many of the earlier railway buildings line this private street. Above the entrance, an iron gate announces TRANSCONA SHOPS, but the site is off limits without special permission to enter. Outside the gates at this intersection are two of the earlier places of accommodation for the workers: a boarding house next to Transcona Television and the Pandora Inn, originally the Palma Hotel. The Transcona Historical Museum is in the 1926 Bank of Toronto building a block away. The town's oldest bank, however, is the former Canadian Bank of Commerce, the prairie standby, built in 1915. Both are located on Regent Street.[3]

REGINA

As the CPR continued building its tracks westward, it originally intended to cross the Wascana Creek farther north, closer to Fort Qu'Appelle, where a Hudson's Bay post had already attracted the nucleus of a small settlement. However, after land speculators had acquired many of the key properties, the CPR — with no fanfare — moved the alignment farther south to Pile o' Bones Creek, so-named for the mass slaughter of buffalo in the area, now Wascana Creek (the name is from the Cree word *Oskana*, meaning "bones"). The flatter terrain here promised to make track-laying easier.

Another factor was Edgar Dewdney, lieutenant governor for the Northwest Territories, who made the decision to relocate the capital of the territories from Battleford to the new railway alignment. It may only be coincidence that Dewdney was part of a syndicate that owned a nearby parcel of land, but this drove the railway to actually locate its station site farther north from the creek where Dewdney's land was located. Dewdney nonetheless chose the creek as the location of the new legislative buildings and his official residence. Finally, the railway further snubbed the landowners of Regina by rejecting it as its divisional point in favour of Moose Jaw.

SASKATOON

Saskatoon's origins lay not with the railways but with the temperance movement. In 1883, responding to government incentives to settle the west, a Methodist temperance group boarded a train and headed for Moose Jaw, and from there they travelled north to the banks of the North Saskatchewan River and created their temperance community.

In 1898 the first railway arrived in the form of the Qu'Appelle, Long Lake and Saskatchewan Railway (QLL&S), which located its station on the other side of the river from the existing settlement. Naturally, growth shifted to site of the station. In 1906 the CNo assumed control of the QLL&S and began to build its line from Saskatoon to Calgary, locating its Saskatoon station at the west end of 2nd Street. The CNR later replaced the building, adding the castle-like Bessborough Hotel at the opposite end of the street. In 1908 the CPR arrived and established a village known as Sutherland. It would then cross the North Saskatchewan River on a high level bridge and build a grand station. With rail lines converging on the booming community, Saskatoon developed into a major rail hub.

However, urban sprawl beginning in the 1950s has greatly diminished the influence of the railway on the city's landscape. In the 1960s, the CNR relocated its downtown station to the fringes of the city, and in its original place now stands a downtown mall. The facade of the mall is a replica of the Canadian Northern station. It faces east along 2nd Street, where the CNR's former Bessborough Hotel dominates. In between, a number of heritage businesses line the street, which itself has been turned into a pedestrian mall featuring cafes and restaurants, with streetscaping such as benches and trees.

EDMONTON

Alberta's capital did not have its origins rooted in the railways. Fort Edmonton, on the South Saskatchewan River, was established for the fur trade, and travel was by steamer on the river. When the Calgary and Edmonton Railway did arrive, it located its station on the south side of the river, around which the town of Strathcona developed. Here, in 1891, the CPR (then the Calgary and Edmonton Railway) added several buildings at Whyte and 103rd Street, including the station, section houses, engine house, and a hotel called the Edmonton House. It was renamed in 1899 when the town changed its own name from South Edmonton to Strathcona.

It was not until 1913, when the high level bridge crossed the deep valley, that the CPR added a new urban station at Jasper Avenue and 109th Street in Edmonton itself. Earlier, the CNo's builders, Mackenzie and Mann, had obtained the charter of the Edmonton, Yukon and Pacific Railway, using it to obtain federal funding for a bridge across the river to link the C&E with Edmonton.

In 1905 the CNo had completed its own line from Winnipeg and built a station at 101st Street and 104th Avenue, with its yards to the west of that location. In 1928 the CNR replaced that classic station with a more modern structure, which in 1966 gave way to a CN office tower nicknamed the "CN Tower."

All evidence of Edmonton's earlier railway heritage has gone from the downtown. The CPR tore down its station in 1978 and the CN has relocated its office tower operations to the Walker yards. Only the Hotel Macdonald, at the south end of 101st Street, reminds us of Edmonton's once-vital days of rail.

With the removal of the CPR tracks over the High Level Bridge in 1995, Strathcona has reverted to its role as the CPR's northern terminal and has once more become Edmonton's main display of railway heritage. Here, the 1908 CPR station still dominates the townscape with its prominent polygonal tower above the operator's bay window. Close by, the historic Strathcona Hotel complements the station's railway heritage. Much of the downtown core, too, dates to the days when Strathcona grew with the railway. A replica of the first C&E station is located on 86th Avenue and houses a museum. Even the CPR itself has constructed a new crew facility south of the station in a style which is reminiscent of a heritage station.

All of this heritage was threatened in the 1970s when the city proposed a short-sighted plan to level much of the old town to build a freeway to Edmonton. In response, the citizens formed the Old Strathcona Foundation and succeeded in having the area, with thirty heritage structures, designated a heritage district. In addition, fourteen additional properties have received individual designations. As a result, Old Strathcona has become a busy attraction for tourists and locals alike. A railway heritage lives on.

LETHBRIDGE

Despite its heavy dependence on the CPR, Lethbridge owes its origins to what lay beneath: coal. The early Siksika First Nations people knew of the exposed seam, calling it the "black rocks." As Canada's first finance minister, Alexander Galt was anxious to encourage settlers to move to what were then called the Northwest Territories. His son, Elliot Torrance Galt, familiar with the outcropping, urged his father to open a mine.

In 1881 Galt founded the Northwestern Coal and Navigation Company to begin the operation. First known as Coalbanks, the community grew and became the town of Lethbridge. The coal was at first shipped out by steamer, but the shallow waters made that method somewhat perilous. To facilitate the movement, the CPR arrived in 1905 and established a divisional point in Lethbridge with one the Prairies' most impressive railway stations. Today, Lethbridge has evolved into southwestern Alberta's main city, offering health, educational, and municipal services to a wide area of the province. While the CPR maintains a yard in Kipp, north of the city, the grand station has become a health centre. It and the soaring railway trestle over the Oldman River have become heritage landmarks and celebrate the former prominence of the CPR.

MOOSE JAW

To confound the land speculators in Regina, the CPR rejected the new territorial capital as a divisional point and opted instead for Moose Jaw, sixty kilometres to the west. With its several hundred kilometres of yard tracks, Moose Jaw had no fewer than ten rail lines radiating out at its peak. The Italianate 1928 CPR station, the third on the site, with its grand tower and plaza, dominated the main street and the urban skyline.

Such a town, with a large and virile male population, naturally invited members of the world's oldest profession to set up shop, and River Street, a block north of the station, grew into a row of well-frequented hotels, among them the Brunswick Hotel.[4]

During the 1990s, the city council designated the Brunswick, Moose Jaw's oldest hotel, as a heritage property and installed decorative sidewalks and street lighting, as well as a wrought-iron gateway, to announce the entrance to River Street's historic hotel row. But in some communities, development can trump heritage, and the plans of a developer to erect a boutique hotel convinced the town that heritage didn't matter, and the historic block of hotels was demolished. As of late 2011, River Street remained a

Moose Jaw's main street remains dominated by the CPR station.

series of parking lots, although the iron gate and decorative light standards still stand bizarrely in place.

Tunnels discovered beneath the streets fueled speculation that they either were part of a prohibition-era rum-running operation (Moose Jaw was linked to Capone-era Chicago by means of the Soo Line) or were hideaways for Chinese railway workers. And so, to promote this unexpected story, the city now offers "Tunnels of Moose Jaw" tours with the nearby "Capone's Hideaway" Motel, a '30s-era bus, and a Capone-style yellow Rolls-Royce automobile to round out the image.

Although the CPR's grand station has closed its doors to passenger service, it is now "Station Square," dominated by a liquor store, and still stands grandly at the end of the main street. Beyond the station, the CPR still maintains an extensive area of sorting yards, although fewer lines radiate from the city now.

CALGARY

Before the CPR arrived on the banks of the Bow River, Calgary was little more than a small settlement clustered around Fort Calgary. The first railway station was added a distance away from the settlement, forcing the few merchants at the fort to uproot and re-establish themselves by the station. That first building was a mere converted boxcar but was quickly replaced with a more substantial structure. In 1912 the CPR established its Ogden yards across the Bow River, and the city became a major repair centre for the railway.

Downtown, the CPR added is elegant Palliser Hotel, beside which it built a solid three-storey station, the fourth on the site. A busy downtown evolved along Stephen Avenue, two blocks from the station. When that station was removed, passenger service moved into the ground level of the hotel.

Neither the CNo nor the GTP built stations of their own, moving instead into existing structures — the CNo into a Catholic parish hall and the GTP into a Mountie barracks. With the elimination of VIA Rail's passenger service by the Mulroney government in 1990, the station facilities closed down. Today, tourists board the magnificent *Royal Canadian Pacific* tour train through a new facility in the renovated former post office. The CNo station still stands but is now a ballet school, although its former role had no influence on the urban form around it.

The Palliser Hotel still offers luxury accommodation, while the earlier station grounds are now the site of the Calgary Tower. Stephen Avenue continues to reflect its roots in Calgary's rail-related growth and is now a designated heritage district. Here, a pedestrian mall passes historic structures, and heritage plaques recount those early days of rail.

The Ghost Towns

The prairie towns were born of the railways and died with them. They dotted the main lines and the branch lines every ten to fifteen kilometres. Most of the smaller communities remained utterly dependent upon the trains that carried their residents to visit other towns, that carried their mail, and most importantly that hauled their grain. Even after the Canadian National Railway took over the failed Grand Trunk Pacific and Canadian Northern Railway lines, it added still more branch lines.

Depression and drought, however, took their toll, and branch lines began to become uneconomical. But the big move to abandon rail operations came in the 1950s and 60s with the switch to diesel from coal and the advent of automated signalling. Larger grain companies moved to more centralized terminals, and many of the elevators fell into disuse. Improved roads turned most people to cars and away from rail travel. All of these factors combined to doom the little railway towns, and very quickly they shriveled to a mere handful of people or emptied completely.

Strewn across the Prairies and along the vacant rail beds, there today lies a litany of ghost towns too numerous to list in this volume, although there are some concentrations. The southern portions of Saskatchewan harbour what may even be considered a "ghost town" line, with a string of such desolate places. Others stand out for retaining a certain railway feature, such as a grain elevator or even a station.

To celebrate the ghost town heritage of the Prairies, however, is too painful for those who had to surrender homes, businesses, friends, and indeed even lifestyles, and few places wish to acknowledge their status. Proposals by the "Harper" government to kill the wheat board will create even more. Surprisingly, then, there are some that have chosen to promote their ghost towns.

ALBERTA
Heinsburg

This quiet hamlet, on the banks of the North Saskatchewan River north of Lloydminister, bills itself as Alberta's "liveliest" ghost town. It is a community that has been working to celebrate its railway heritage. While the main street of empty storefronts puts it in the "ghost town" category, the preservation of both the village station and the wooden railway water tower underlie a lively community.

Heinsburg began life as a ferry crossing. It was not until 1928, however, well after the Canadian National Railway had taken over the bankrupt Canadian Northern, that the tracks finally reached Heinsburg, making it that line's terminus. With its two grain elevators, Heinsburg

grew into a focal point for the many First Nations and European settlements to the north and east.

Dieselization put the tower out of use in the 1960s, and road improvements rendered the line itself uneconomical, and, in 1983, the tracks were lifted. Today, the community is a terminus of a different sort, being the jumping-off point for the popular Iron Horse Rail Trail (described in a different chapter). Partly as a result, the water tower and the 1950s-era Canadian National railway station are preserved on their original sites. Meanwhile, lurking on the once main street, the sagging ghostly shells of former businesses remind us of Heinsburg's days as a vital rail terminal.

"Rowleywood"

The ghost town of Rowley in central Alberta gave itself this ironic nickname because of its role in such Hollywood blockbusters as *Bye Bye Blues* and in various documentaries and commercials. The quiet community has only a few occupied homes, while the main street buildings, although vacant, are kept in repair. In fact, the last Saturday of each month, the community hosts a pizza night. The town has also managed to retain its Canadian Northern railway station and three Alberta Wheat Pool grain elevators. Buildings that formerly served as a bank and hospital still stand on these silent streets, and the site is now known as the Yesteryear Artifacts Museum.

Wayne

Tucked into the gullies of Alberta's Drumheller badlands, Wayne may not declare itself to be a ghost town, but it doesn't hide the fact either. What remains of its once busy main streets lies scenically at the foot of the layered, eroded wall of Rose Deer Valley. Here, in 1912, the Rose Deer Coal Mining Company began to access the coal deposits, which were intermingled with the ancient eroded bedrock of the badlands. Soon, the town of Wayne could count 1,500 residents, most of them working at the coal mines. A small station stood by the tracks, which ran down the main street. By the 1930s, the coal mines were closing down, and by the 1950s, only a handful of residents remained in the town. But the still-functioning Rose Deer Hotel's cowboy-style Last Chance Saloon, with its prairie-style facade, contains photos that recount the town's early heyday.

The authenticity of the saloon and street has lured Hollywood filmmakers to the site, including the makers of *Shanghai Noon*, starring Jackie Chan. Each summer, the ghost town comes to life for the Wayne motorcycle rally. Otherwise-empty streets and a few scattered homes and cabins remain, as do a few samples of railway equipment from the coal-mining days.

One of the more scenic of the prairie ghost towns is the former coal town of Wayne, lying below the gullies of the Drumheller Badlands.

Dorothy

Of the thirty-four working coal mines and more than 130 registered mines in the Drumheller Valley — mines which yielded fifty-seven million tons of coal — the best preserved is the Atlas Coal Mine. It closed in 1979 and is now a National Historic Site. Here, the old structures and equipment adorn the museum and interpretive centre.

At the ghost town of Dorothy, a derelict grain elevator rises above the valley floor. When the CPR arrived in the 1920s, Dorothy grew to 150 residents and contained a station, store, school, two churches, and three grain elevators. Those photogenic churches are set against a backdrop of the colourful layers of the eroded Badlands gullies, while most of the few village streets are now silent. Dorothy is sometimes described as one of Alberta's most photogenic ghost towns.

Endiang

This "almost" ghost town near Hanna celebrated its one hundred years of existence in 2010 by erecting a heritage

Heinsburg bills itself as a "lively" ghost town, due to its successful efforts to preserve the station and water tower.

plaque along its quiet streets. One of the few structures to survive the rail lines' closure is the Endiang Trading Company, which existed from 1925 to 1982. Today, it has become the Our Home Kitchen tea room and is the only early building to remain on what was once a bustling main street, which was dominated by a two-storey CNR station at the end. The grain elevator lasted until 1983 and was the hamlet's last link with its rail roots. The railway roadbed today is only scarcely visible.

The elevators are now gone, as is most of the main street, leaving it with a ghost-town look.

Retlaw

Here is another example of a ghost town that seems to celebrate its heritage. "Retlaw" is *Walter* spelled backwards, to honour the CPR official Walter Baker. By the 1920s, the town's main street could boast of a pool hall, hotel, shops, and a station. But the nearby town of Vauxhall was closer to a new irrigation project, and Retlaw fell silent, with nothing left today save a small handful of vacant buildings and foundations. The church has been restored, and many foundations now have historic plaques to help visitors visualize the town's heyday and appreciate its heritage.

MANITOBA

Mowbray

This little Manitoba ghost town on the North Dakota border is at the end of the line in more ways than one. In 1902 a branch of the CPR extended to this border, where it built one of its large Western Line Stations. Opposite the tracks was a modest main street of boomtown-style stores and a pair of grain elevators. Children from North Dakota would stroll across the unfenced border to attend Mowbray's Boundary School and then back home for lunch. The little main street also contained a general store, blacksmith's shop, pool room, barber shop, and dance hall. The Mowbray Hotel, which stood near the station, did a booming business with train passengers, especially during the days of U.S. prohibition. However, American border patrols, combined with the local temperance movement, brought business to a standstill.

During the 1930s, train service was reduced to one per week and then abandoned altogether. Today, all that remains are three vacant houses and, surprisingly, the station, which is now a neatly tended dwelling, still displaying the CPR red paint and the hand-painted name on the end. Even though children no longer cross the border to attend Mowbray's school, it survives today as a provincial heritage landmark, its furnishings still intact. Opened in 1887, class was finally dismissed in 1956. But don't wander too close to the invisible border with our southern neighbours — you may find yourself peering up at a Homeland Security helicopter, even in a Manitoba ghost town.

Port Nelson

At 810 kilometres in length, the Hudson Bay Railway has been around since the 1930s and carries the many vital supplies that the roadless communities in northern Manitoba require, as well as more major commodities such as wheat and mining and petroleum products.

Having an ocean port on Hudson's Bay had long been an ambition of both the Manitoba and Canadian governments, but controversy swirled over whether the port would be located at Churchill, the present location, or at Port Nelson. While Churchill was farther and tundra needed to be crossed, Port Nelson offered a superior townsite but an inferior harbour. In 1912 the federal government of Robert Borden decided on Port Nelson and work began the following year. To help overcome the harbour limitations, an artificial island was built and a seventeen-span trestle extended to it. Port Nelson became a busy construction camp, with upwards of one thousand workers housed in its bunkhouses.

By 1918 the war had halted any further construction. With costs of constructing the port climbing to a staggering $6.5 million, an inquiry in 1919 learned that, despite the decision of the government, the project engineer had never approved of Port Nelson as the terminus. In 1927 the government reversed its decision and chose Churchill instead. By 1928 Port Nelson had become a ghost town, with the engineering office, wireless building, and several homes standing vacant. Meanwhile, the port of Churchill was completed in 1929 and trains began running in 1931. Today at Port Nelson, concrete wharfs, foundations, and a seventeen-span trestle still stand as a testimony to the folly of the original decision.

The CPR's Ghost Town Line

It has been said by ghost-town hunters that to find such places one need only to follow a prairie branch line. While that may be a hit-and-miss endeavour, there is one line that does yield a greater abundance of abandoned places, and that is a southern CPR line that stretched from Souris in Manitoba to Stirling in Alberta.

Construction began in Souris in 1890 and continued to Reston, where a former CPR engine house yet stands. Then, from Reston, the route continued in 1900, reaching Forward and Assiniboia in 1910. By 1914 it had reached Attawan in southwestern Saskatchewan. The western section had been completed from Stirling to Manyberries in 1915, with the final link being broached in 1922. With rolling grasslands and cattle ranches,

the route was not particularly profitable, and by the early 2000s, no tracks remained between Foremost and Consul. The lifting of the tracks and the disappearance of the grain elevators resulted in many of the little railway communities withering, many disappearing altogether.

In Saskatchewan, some of the more photogenic ghost towns include Maleval, Mayronne, Khedive, and Vidora, which had its own electrical grid and now consists of a pair of vacant structures on private land. Robsart could boast of its own hospital, town, council, and thirty businesses. The vacant hospital still stands, as do a number of abandoned main street stores. Being close to the American border, Senate and Govenlock enjoyed a brief period of prosperity during the days of prohibition. Whiskey would arrive by train to the Govenlock Hotel, which held a festive occasion known as the Bootleggers Ball. Today, only a plaque survives to mark the town. Scotsguard has fared a little better. Known as "Little Chicago," it could once boast a population of 350, with a hotel, theatre, town hall, and six elevators. That had plunged to six residents by 1987. A few derelict buildings, including a church, are scattered among the vacant streets.

Manyberries, Alberta, while described by some as a "ghost town," remains a populated place. The station, restored as a house with track and a caboose in front, still stands at the end of a now nearly vacant main street, although the Ranchman's Inn can still offer lodging and a meal. The area's ranching heritage is reflected in the many cattle brands that decorate the inn's walls. Orion, the next on the line, used to boast of a main street with three general stores, a pool hall and hotel, as well as grain elevators. Today, Orion provides many vacant buildings and overgrown lots, as does Nemiskam, while Skiff and Wrentham fall within the "partial" ghost town category. Notably, Skiff retains its elevator, where a string of boxcars and a caboose stand on a siding. Foremost, today's eastern end of rail, serves as a busy regional centre. (It is worth pausing in Etzikam, not a ghost town, to view the rather unusual windmill museum).

With the abandonment of hundreds of kilometres of branch lines and the removal of the elevators, nearly every rail line can count dozens of ghost towns, or hamlets that resemble them, with overgrown streets, vacant false-fronted stores, and sagging houses. Few prairie ghost towns retain any component of their railway roots.

The main street of Manyberries, Alberta, still ends at the back door of its preserved CPR station.

However, lurking within a few of these ghostly remnants — places in Saskatchewan like Alvena, Jedburgh, and Parkerview — are grain elevators and stations. Mowbray in Manitoba and Manyberries, Heinsburg, and Rowley in Alberta are ghost towns, or partially so, and they retain their stations in their original locations. In Saskatchewan, grain elevators still stand silently in ghost towns like Fusilier, Sovereign, Bents, and Peterson; in Alberta, Rowley and Dorothy; and Brandenwarden in Manitoba.

Heritage Towns

All across the Prairies, a number of railway towns are becoming heritage attractions on their own, communities like Radville, Vilna, Strathcona, Ogema, and Empress. In Alberta more than two dozen communities have undertaken main street upgrades under that province's Main Street program. Manitoba's Hometown Main Street Enhancements program helps fund streetscape improvements in communities across that province. In April 2011, the province of Saskatchewan announced a similar program. Although such improvements may not necessarily incorporate rail heritage features, nearly all main streets in the Prairies owed their origins to the railways and the stations that stood at the foot of those streets. Some of the more exciting heritage communities are listed here.

EMPRESS, ALBERTA

Located in the Badlands of Alberta, Empress began as a CPR divisional town on what became known as the "Empress" line, named in honour of the late Queen Victoria, who had been the empress of India. With its small but distinctive station and divisional facilities, the town developed into a busy community. But the station closed in 1972, and the tracks were lifted a few years later. The town was on the verge of becoming a ghost town.

Then, it was "discovered." A number of artists have located their studios here or nearby. Sagebrush Studios has moved three historic churches onto its property to serve as additional studios. Another, the Knarls and Knots studio, features handmade furniture. The most active of the new businesses is "That's Empressive" — a tea room and gift shop situated in the former Bank of Commerce, which was built in 1919 and remained in business until the CPR closed its divisional point operations; for a time it served as a boarding house. The TD moved into the building, which remained a bank until 1997, when a jeweller bought it for

his studio. The building was then purchased by Pat and Ross Donaldson to sell artwork. Since then it has become the focus of the community, with its tea room and gift items, as well as being the town's only convenience store.[5]

VILNA, ALBERTA

Shortly after taking over the CNo and the GTP, the newly formed CNR began to expand into the area northeast of Edmonton to help open the area to settlement, especially for soldiers returning from the First World War. At the site of today's Vilna, the CNR established a station and a community quickly grew. The main street contained a hardware store, bank, hotel, post office, and a pool hall, among other businesses.

Radville's main street contains a heritage bank and a heritage hotel, as well as the preserved station at the end of the street.

Despite the removal of the railway line, Vilna's main street has remained largely intact. In fact, so much so that the Alberta Main Street Program has helped fund the street's revitalization. More than twenty main street buildings have been improved or fully restored, many dating back to the village's boom years in the 1920s to the early '30s.

But the best known of the main street buildings is the pool hall and barbershop. Built in 1921 by Steve Pawluk, it remained in use as a pool hall and barber shop until 1996. In that year, it was purchased by the Friends of the Vilna Pool Hall and Barbershop Historical Society, who succeeded in having it declared a provincial heritage property. The interior still retains its barber shop and pool hall fixtures, making it Alberta's oldest pool hall. Although no railway structures have survived, the railway right of way forms part of the popular Iron Horse rail trail. Vilna's heritage main street attracts many day-use visitors from places like Edmonton. It goes to show that heritage, when preserved, can be an economical benefit — a notion too many prairie communities don't seem to get.

OLD STRATHCONA, ALBERTA

The Old Strathcona heritage district of Edmonton owes its origins to the 1891 refusal of the CPR to build its Calgary and Edmonton line over the South Saskatchewan River. As a result, the town grew up around the CPR station and its yards. The CNo acquired the charter of the Edmonton, Yukon and Pacific Railway and built the "low level" bridge over the river, finally connecting tracks on both sides. With the opening of the High Level bridge in 1913, the CPR itself crossed the mighty valley and built its own station in Edmonton, and Strathcona became part of the city.

Many of the early buildings have survived, and today five city blocks have been designated as a heritage district, with a number of buildings along Whyte Avenue dating from the railway's heyday. Nearly two dozen individual buildings are designated as well, including the Gainers Block, the Princess Theatre, the old post office, and the Douglas Block.

Two of the more prominent structures are the Strathcona Hotel, built in 1891 as the Edmonton House, and the massive CPR station itself, built in 1909. With its polygonal tower above the operator's bay, it was one of only five like it across the Prairies. A replica of the first C&E station is now a museum on 86th Avenue NW and contains a working telegraph, just as was used when the original station was in operation. Similarly, Okotoks has revitalized its "Old Town" and has incorporated a gallery and tourism office into its unusual CPR station, located on North Railway Street.

OGEMA, SASKATCHEWAN

This community began around 1912, when the CPR laid its tracks through the area and planned the site for a town. Since it was the end of the tracks at that time, the inhabitants decided on *Omega* as a name, as that is the last letter in the Greek alphabet. However, a post office already had that name, and so, with a minor shift in letters, it became *Ogema*, which is also the Cree word for "big chief."

Ogema is a town that actively celebrates its roots. In addition to a CPR station, which has been relocated from a farm back to the end of the main street, many heritage buildings line the main street, including a rare example of a brick firewall halfway along. This was built following a devastating fire in 1915 in order to prevent future fires from spreading so rapidly. Opposite is a brick fire station, erected in part for the same reason. One of the more unusual structures, another rare building, is a 1925 BA "filling" station, now a municipal heritage property. The 1923 butcher store is now the C & C Supermarket. The station will become the boarding point for Saskatchewan's newest tour train on the Southern Prairie Railway.

RADVILLE, SASKATCHEWAN

Here in southern Saskatchewan lies yet another heritage treasure: Radville, with historic buildings lining a main street that ends, as it should, at the back of the CNo station. In 1909 the CNo, which was busily building yet another of its branch lines, chose Radville as a divisional point. It erected a water tower, roundhouse, and a standard class-2 divisional-point station. (The railways classified their stations by the importance of their functions. A class 2 was a larger "divisional" station with sorting yards and maintenance facilities, as well as the usual waiting rooms.)

In choosing Radville, the CNo bypassed another community, Brooking, which had hoped to attract the divisional functions. Today, that community is a vanished ghost town. While the Radville station has become a museum, a number of other heritage buildings stand as well. Most prominent among them is the Canadian Bank of Commerce, now the CIBC. It was prefabricated in British Columbia and assembled in Radville in 1911. Across the street, the Empire Hotel, now the Long Creek Saloon, dates to the same year. The Radville Senior Citizens club occupies what was the Province Theatre, built in 1925, which lost its second floor as a result of a fire in 1943. The tourism office on the main street has prepared a walking tour of this historic railway town.

ROULEAU, SASKATCHEWAN

While Rouleau still retains a grain elevator, it is not the town's name that appears on the side. Rather it is "Dog River," the name that made Rouleau famous. In 2003 Tisdale-born comedian Brent Butt and CTV location scouts selected this prairie town as the setting for the popular TV sitcom *Corner Gas*. And it fills the bill. With its grain elevator, its flat treeless prairie landscape, and a modest main street, it became Canada's ultimate typical prairie town. Although the cast and crew have since departed, the grain elevator has retained its fictional name, as have at least two of the iconic fictional buildings on the main street, namely the "Dog River Hotel" and the "police station." *Corner Gas* aficionados continue to arrive at the police station, which is now a snack bar and gift shop selling Corner Gas paraphernalia. The set, with the gas station and The Ruby diner, was still there in late 2011, but it's actually a kilometre west of the town, and The Ruby's sign is now in the gift shop. Rouleau itself developed along the CPR's Soo Line in 1895 and prospered thanks to the high quality of the surrounding farm land. The former Rouleau CPR station is now a residence on a village side street.

Corner Gas fans will recognize these Rouleau landmarks as being the set for the popular TV show.

Chapter Three

The Stations

The local nerve centres of the railways were the stations. They served many more functions than today's generation could imagine, and the man (usually) in charge was the railway station agent. Therefore, one of the building's main roles was to house the agent and his family, and this was almost always in an upstairs or rear apartment. The agent had to issue passenger tickets, as well as organize (and often solicit) freight shipments. To keep the trains moving, he issued train orders by "hooping" them up to the engineer on a long curved or forked stick known as a hoop. He also fixed the signal in front of the station to indicate to the engineer if he needed to slow down, stop, or continue through. Preparing the mail sack was still another duty for the agent, as many trains contained a mail sorting car right on board.

Agents also enjoyed a more aesthetic role — maintaining the station garden. Some of the earliest and largest gardens were those laid out beside the stations in Regina, Medicine Hat, Moose Jaw, and Calgary. The CPR's first nursery was established at Wolesley, Saskatchewan, under the direction of Gustaf Bosson Krook, a Swedish-born horticulturist who held the position for twenty years. During the First World War, the gardens switched from flowers to vegetables, and after the Second World War, to parking lots. Between the wars, greenhouses in Winnipeg, Calgary, and Moose Jaw were providing 125 different varieties of flowers and shrubs.

While a community's first station was more likely than not to be either a converted boxcar or passenger coach, Canada's railways quickly got down to building more substantial stations. How big depended upon the business emanating or projected from that location. Once the designs became more elaborate, the railway station became the signature of the rail line that was building it, which each line having distinctive patterns.

The CPR was the first railway to cross the Prairies. In its haste to reach the Pacific coast, which was the goal behind the company's creation, it very quickly erected stations. Its first president, William Cornelius Van Horne, sent a common station plan to contractors along the line: a very simple full two-storey building with gable ends, usually with a single storey freight wing. These served for twenty years or so until the CPR, to attract more business, devised a greater variety of more aesthetically pleasing station designs, primarily for small-town way stations.

Many of these stations owe their appearance to Ralph Benjamin Pratt, the CPR's main architect from 1898 to 1901, at which point he was hired away by the Canadian Northern Railway. He came up with two of the CPR's more interesting styles. One such design, displaying an attractive mansard-style roof, appeared largely in Manitoba, although several were built along the CPR's Calgary and Edmonton line and the Qu'Appelle, Long Lake and

Saskatchewan lines. Rosthern, Saskatchewan; Didsbury, Alberta; and La Riviere, Manitoba, are surviving examples of the twenty such structures that were built on the prairies. Another of his classic styles consisted of a high pyramid above a second storey and featured pagoda-style flourishes on the roof tip and gables. Of twenty-two such CPR stations, sixteen were built in Manitoba.

With the next style the CPR introduced, in 1905, Pratt's absence was noticeable. The first of these designs, which the CPR designated as "Standard # 5" and "Standard #10" (the only difference being in the size), appeared in 128 communities in Alberta and Saskatchewan. Consisting of a simple two-storey structure, the design's only embellishment was a hip gable above a pair of second-storey windows.

In 1909 the CPR came up with the Western Line Stations (WLS), which were built exclusively across the Prairies. This style, known as "A-2 WLS," was similar to its predecessor stations, the main difference being that the front gable on the second storey was peaked rather than hipped, and nearly all were built in Alberta and

This station in Theodore, Saskatchewan, was designed by R.B. Pratt and is one of the CPR's more interesting designs, with its pagoda-like features.

Saskatchewan (172 of 197 were found in these provinces). This style also appeared later, along the CPR's new Toronto to Sudbury main line in Ontario.

This era of simpler stations was followed in the period of 1920–30, when the CPR introduced its A-3 WLS, which is considered to one of that line's more interesting stations. Again the stations were two storeys in height, and the designers decided to bring the front gable down the full width of the second-storey facade. Sixty-one were built between 1920 and 1930, most along the new Lanigan to Melfort line and as replacement stations in Manitoba. A half-dozen survive, largely as museums or private homes.

But as the 1920s wound down, and the auto age diminished the prominence of the country station, the CPR's final station design marked a return to simplicity. Erected between 1924 and 1931 in sixty-two locations, mostly on new branch lines, it was a two-storey structure with the second level appearing as a large dormer. A wide, sweeping roofline added a pleasing flourish to the building. Several of these now serve as museums.

Ogema's "new" station displays one of the CPR's most common and more simple styles introduced following the departure of R.B. Pratt.

Many stations were designed for divisional points, where more staff needed to be accommodated. These structures were surprisingly small, but in such locations, staff accommodation could usually be found in the community. A particularly pleasing style was allocated to more than a dozen divisional points throughout Alberta and Saskatchewan. This design consisted of only a single storey, and a large flared gable dominated the roof, both front and back, while a wide wrap-around eave displayed a similarly flared roof. The front entrance was by means of a porte-cochère, again with a flared roof.

Finally, the grandest designs were reserved for the largest towns and cities. The popular Richardsonian Romanesque style influenced the CPR's then-architect Edwin Colonna in places like Calgary, Swift Current, Regina (preceding the current building), and Portage la Prairie. The stations in Lethbridge, Strathcona, Medicine Hat, Red Deer, and Saskatoon all followed a common Château-style influence, while those grand urban terminals in Winnipeg, Brandon, and Regina were all custom-designed along neo-classical lines, using arches and pillars to mark the entrances. Altogether the CPR

With this station style at Oxbow, Saskatchewan, the CPR began to reintroduce more aesthetically pleasing buildings.

erected nearly 1,200 stations — more than half in Saskatchewan — roughly one third were portables.

The Canadian Northern Railway, which was building as many branch lines as it could as inexpensively as possible, came up with a mere three different styles. Created by CNo architect Ralph Benjamin Pratt — who, as mentioned, was lured from the CPR in 1901 — these designs included the common wayside station, which was a storey-and-a-half with a steep pyramid roof and a prominent dormer to represent the location of the agent's quarters. The effect was pronounced, as these high roofs

could be easily seen for a great distance, especially on the flat, treeless landscape — a design element which was intentional. These structures were labeled as "class 3" stations. Between 1901 and 1924, 293 CNo 3rd class stations were built (a few were also constructed by the CNR using the former plans), with 145 in Saskatchewan, sixty-nine in Alberta, and sixty-two in Manitoba.

Less important locations received single storey structures, where the agent might enjoy only a small apartment at the rear. Known as "class 4" stations, hundreds still stand, though most were relocated to become homes or museums.

The station in Outlook, Saskatchewan, now a museum, shows the divisional style of station used by the CPR across the prairies.

Divisional stations were likewise identical. While sporting the iconic pyramid roof, they were also given wings on each end of the main building, and these, too, would include dormer windows on the second level. Many of these survive, including several on site.

Between 1901 and 1916, the CNo constructed sixteen 2nd-class divisional stations in the Prairies, with five in Alberta and four in both Manitoba and Saskatchewan.

A small handful of grander custom-designed stations appeared in places like Dauphin, Manitoba (still standing); Saskatoon (removed, but a replica was later built); and Edmonton. Regina's station became a union station with the CPR, and the Winnipeg station joined the Grand Trunk Pacific Railway in building an exemplary union station there.

The third main line, the Grand Trunk Pacific, similarly kept its variety of station styles to a minimum. For the most part, it applied only two patterns to its way stations, and even those were nearly identical. Those country stations displayed attractive little

The station at Cudworth, Saskatchewan, was a style introduced by the CNR after it took over the CNo's branch lines.

designs, which featured wide overhangs and a bell-cast roof, differing only as to whether they employed an octagonal or square dormer above an octagonal or square operator's bay window. Of those that survive, most have been relocated to become homes or museums. Divisional stations offered more variety, ranging from full two-storey, half-timbered structures, such as that still standing in Melville to those with more prominent dormers. This line created 206 small town and rural stations.

The successor to the GTP and the CNo, namely the Canadian National Railway, while not needing to add many new stations, kept them simple — usually a full two storeys with little flair or embellishment. Towns with examples still standing on site include, in Saskatchewan, Glaslyn, Frenchman's Butte, and Cudworth. After the CNR entered the picture, it added a further 103 stations in the towns and villages of the Prairies.[6]

The Big Valley station is the kind that the CNo used at their prairie divisional points. Along with the grain elevator, it presents a heritage railway landscape.

Saving the Stations

By the mid 1950s, railways were switching from coal-fired steam locomotives to those powered by diesel, and this dramatically altered the railway landscape of the Prairies. As diesels could travel farther and faster without refueling, every other divisional point shut down. Roundhouses, coal docks, and water towers no longer served a purpose, and centralized traffic control eliminated the need for station operators to pass along train orders to the engineers. In addition, the CN and CP introduced centralized service operations to process freight orders and shipping, and many station agents became redundant.

Then, with the end of the mail contracts and a sharp decline in passenger travel — thanks to the ever-present automobile — more stations went quiet. The decade that followed witnessed the elimination of 80 percent of the railway stations across the Prairies and indeed throughout the country. Of the nearly two thousand stations built

Although less glamorous than steam engines, diesels such as these on display in Medicine Hat hold considerable aesthetic appeal.

across the three prairie provinces, only 720 remained as of the mid-90s, the last time a station census took place.[7] More than 90 percent of these had been dragged off to become barns, private homes, or restaurants. Only a small handful remained on site.

Farsighted municipalities saw the risk of losing their heritage and gobbled up the old buildings, primarily for museums but also for libraries and seniors drop-in centres. Regrettably, the railway companies usually forced the purchaser to remove the building from the station grounds, and all too many were ignored and demolished. The mass extermination these cherished heritage buildings, especially in the Prairies' towns and villages, which would not have existed at all were it not for train stations, led to an outcry across the country. In 1988 the federal government passed into law the Heritage Railway Station Protection Act. Once designated as a protected structure under the act, a station could not be demolished or even significantly altered. In less than ten years, the environment minister, responsible for the legislation, granted more than 300 stations this designation.

In Saskatchewan, designated stations included the following:

- Biggar
- Broadview
- Humboldt
- Melville
- Two in Moose Jaw
- North Battleford
- Regina
- Two in Saskatoon
- Swift Current
- Wynyard

Manitoba also had several designated stations:

- Brandon
- Churchill
- Cranberry Portage
- Dauphin
- Emerson
- Gillam
- McCreary
- Minnedosa
- Neepawa
- Two in Portage La Prairie
- Rivers
- Roblin
- St. James
- The Pas
- Virden
- Two in Winnipeg

The following stations in Alberta were also designated:

- Banff
- Empress
- Hanna
- Jasper
- Lake Louise
- Medicine Hat
- Red Deer
- Strathcona

In all, thirty-eight stations have received federal protection across the Prairies. Many others have been designated under provincial statutes or municipal bylaws. Twenty seven stations are listed on Saskatchewan's Register of Heritage Places.

Designations didn't always save them, as many were simply left neglected. Some met their fate at the hands of arsonists, while others simply crumbled into rubble.

Survivors: The Urban Terminals

Many of the major urban terminals that dominated the Prairies' urban landscapes are still around. Few original structures, however, have survived the need to enlarge or upgrade to meet the ever changing needs of the railways. Sadly, grand terminals that stood in places like Calgary and Edmonton are now gone, while the only such structure to still provide rail passenger service is the Union Station in Winnipeg. Others have earned new uses, as in Winnipeg's CPR terminal, which is now an aboriginal centre; Regina's Union Station, now a casino; Lightbridge's CPR station, a health centre; and Saskatoon's CPR station, now a tavern and travel office.

LETHBRIDGE, ALBERTA

In 1895 the CPR extended a line south from of its main line tracks to a small village called Coalbanks in order to tap into the supply of coal in the area. In 1898 the line was further extended to the larger coal seams in the Crowsnest Pass. In 1905 the town of Coalbanks changed its name to Lethbridge. It then encouraged the CPR to relocate its divisional point from Fort Macleod by granting the railway a twenty-year exemption from taxes on 48.6 hectares of land near the downtown. The CPR agreed and built the current station, along with freight sheds and a roundhouse.

Its design is similar to several other such stations across the prairies — such as those in Strathcona, Red Deer, and Saskatoon — and it sports a row of dormers along the former trackside and an iconic octagonal tower on the street side. In 1980 the CPR relocated its yards to Kipp, and the station sat empty. With the redevelopment of downtown Lethbridge, and the relocation of the tracks farther north, the CPR station became a regional health centre and stands today as a designated provincial heritage resource. Despite the absence of tracks, the railway heritage is further enhanced by the placing of CPR steam locomotive *3651* beside what would have been the station's platform and the placing of a caboose at the opposite end. Lethbridge is also the site of one of Canada's most stunning railway trestles.

RED DEER, ALBERTA, CPR STATION

In 1890s, the tracks of the Calgary and Edmonton finally arrived at the south bank of the Red Deer Creek. Although it had meant moving the village's original buildings to trackside, the town of Red Deer began to boom. In 1904 the Canadian Pacific Railway took over the C&E and established Red Deer as a divisional point halfway between Calgary and Edmonton. In 1910 the CP replaced the simpler C&E station with one of their grander designs: built of red brick, the storey-and-a-half structure was topped by a large turret with several hipped dormer windows along the roofline. Divisional tracks sprawled before it, while a large garden with a central foundation was laid out on the streetside entrance. But in 1985, with a major redevelopment occurring in downtown Red Deer, the CPR relocated its tracks and the station became an office building.

WINNIPEG'S UNION STATION

This gateway city to the Canadian Prairies was geographically the convergence of Canada's three major east–west lines. While the CPR was content to enjoy its own station near the city's north end, the CNo and the GTP, along with the GTP's partner the National Transcontinental Railway (NTR), decided to construct a union station to serve both lines. It was, however, the CNo that actually built the structure, with the GTP and NTR as tenants. Accordingly, the CNo engaged the well-known New York firm of Warren and Wetmore to design a grand Beaux-Arts station.

As with many urban stations, the entrance was to be the building's grandest feature. Just as the ancient Greeks and Romans used archways and pillars to mark the grand entrance to their cities, so too did the railway companies for their stations. In the case of the Winnipeg station, the grand arch extends the full three storeys and is topped by a dome. The waiting room, too, reaches the full height of the building and is finished in marble, with arched skylights containing the provincial coats of arms and gold leaf around the walls. While regular passengers could enjoy the amenities of the main hall, arriving immigrants were segregated into their own facilities on the lower level.

Winnipeg's Union station was a collaboration between the CNo and the GTP, and is one of the few functioning stations left on the prairies.

The station still serves VIA Rail passengers travelling on the train named *Canadian* and the Churchill trains. A museum on tracks 1 and 2 contains what is perhaps the most historic piece of railway equipment on the Prairies, the *Countess of Dufferin*, the first steam locomotive to enter service on the Prairies. A walkway leads from the waiting room beneath the tracks to the newly redeveloped Forks complex, where the Manitoba Children's museum is housed in the Northern Pacific and Manitoba Railway engine house and car shop.

WINNIPEG CPR STATION

The CPR's then-main architects, Edward and W.S. Maxwell, chose to incorporate into the Winnipeg station the Beaux-Arts style school of architecture, which was then in vogue. This is a style that also appears in the CPR's Vancouver's station and in Montreal's Windsor Station. The new station in Winnipeg was opened in 1914 and replaced an earlier brick station. Likewise constructed of brick with stone work around the windows and setting off the corners, the grand four-storey entrance is marked

Saskatoon reflects one of the CPR's grand urban styles found predominantly on the prairies.

by two sets of twin pillars embedded in a concrete base. The top of the entrance is richly decorated, and much of the original fixtures still survive in the vast waiting room. Designated both federally and provincially as a heritage structure, the building now houses an aboriginal centre.

SASKATOON CPR

Another of the CPR's grand prairie-chateau stations is that in Saskatoon. Being that city's third rail line, following those of the CNo and GTP, it did not occupy a prominent location in the urban context. It was, however, accompanied by a roundhouse and rail yards, and twenty trains per day passed through the station. The large yellow brick building is two storeys high and displays a fifteen-metre trackside polygonal turret, which incorporates the operator's bay window at track level and extends above the roofline. In 1960 the station was closed, although the CPR continued to use the building as an administrative centre. Finally, the station was vacated in 1972 and efforts for its preservation began. It was designated as a heritage structure under the Heritage Railway Station Protection Act in 1989, one of the first in the country to be so protected, and now houses a variety of businesses along with a grill and restaurant.

SASKATOON CNR

The CNo's first station in Saskatoon was built at the west end of the city's main street, 2nd Street. Later, the CNR would add the Bessborough Hotel at the opposite end of the street. The CNo station sported the line's signature pyramid roof with gabled extensions to each side. The CNR replaced it in the 1930s with a neo-classical building with a flat roof, and it had pillars to mark its two-storey entrance. Later, in 1964, with the CNR looking to the expanding suburbs for clients, where it located today's modern station, the CNR demolished its downtown station.

Saskatoon's new CNR station reflects a more modern heritage. One of the few such post-war stations constructed in Canada, it was built at a time when the CNR was recognizing the role of the automobile. Its location on the western outskirts of the city was intended to appeal to the car-oriented suburban population. It is unusual to consider a building constructed as recently as 1964 to be a heritage resource, but that is nonetheless the case with this station. It was built in what is known as the International style. With its high ceiling and flat roof, and with its ample window area, it is very much the modern station. No longer needed by the CN, its sole remaining function is that of the station stop for VIA Rail's *Canadian*. It was designated as a protected station under the Heritage Railway Station Protection Act in 1996.

STRATHCONA (EDMONTON CPR)

When the Calgary and Edmonton Railway was completed to the south bank of the North Saskatchewan River in 1898, it went no farther, due to the costs of building a major bridge over the river. The first station was a small wooden standard plan CPR station, a replica of which is now a museum in the community of Strathcona. In 1912 the CPR replaced the simple station with one of its grand designs. Because of its status as a terminus, Strathcona grew into a significant-sized town. With a trademark polygonal turret on the building's trackside, the two-storey structure housed waiting rooms, freight offices, and accommodations for the railway staff. The station's walls are brick, while its corners and turrets are clad in Tyndall stone. It resembles other CPR stations in Red Deer, Saskatoon, and Lethbridge. Following the station's closure in 1980, it was converted to a tavern and restaurant.

EDMONTON CNR

The CNR, with R.B. Pratt its architect, built another of its stunning pyramid-roof urban stations. The centre portion was three storeys with a gable dormer front and back and small decorative turrets on the corners. The two wings, of two storeys each, featured three prominent dormers, three windows wide, set into the sweeping bellcast roof. Meanwhile, a wide overhand wrapped around the entire structure. Although the GTP built its own line well to the north of that of the CNo, it began to use the CNo station as well. In 1928 the CNR built a new International-style structure nearby to replace it, although the older station remained until 1952, when it was demolished. The newer building stood at two storeys, with a flat roof and a pair of pillars to guard the entrance. This building, like its predecessor, stood at the north end of 101st Street, looking south toward the Hotel MacDonald. In the 1960s, that structure, too, made way for a CN office and operations building of typical 60s design. It was nicknamed the "CN Tower," and the passenger waiting room was at the ground level.

But even that building no longer houses railway operations. In 2008 the CN removed its operations to the massive Walker railway yards, while VIA Rail, too, vacated the premises for a location adjacent to the City Centre Airport. Its new facility is a bright and spacious structure with a wide awning over the entrance that sports the trademark blue-and-yellow VIA sign. This attractive modernistic building also features Wi-Fi. It is located on 121st Street, just south of the Yellowhead Highway.

MEDICINE HAT (CPR)

The 1906 CPR station in Medicine Hat, Alberta, copied the style found in Strathcona, Red Deer, and the other areas. The building featured the polygonal tower at trackside, with two prominent dormers on the second floor on each side of the tower. By 1911, the yards had become so busy, and the city had grown so quickly, that the station was in effect doubled in length by an identical addition to the east and a large addition between the two.

Today, the yards remain among the railway's busiest, and yet an another addition was added on the street side to accommodate staff and operations. Designated as a heritage structure both federally and provincially, the station retains a number of interior features as well as a portion of its original garden, one of the first such station gardens in western Canada.

CALGARY

Calgary, like Edmonton, had seen its stations come and go. It is hard to believe that its first station was in fact just a converted box car. That was quickly replaced with the more standard "Van Horne" station. It, too, was quickly outdated, and a pair of identical stone structures replaced it. These were wide and single storey. As Calgary continued to grow, it was soon obvious that the city needed something even larger, especially after the opening of the Palliser Hotel in 1914. And so the CPR dismantled the twin stone stations — reconstructing them in High River and Claresholm — and built a large new neo-classical facility east of the hotel. Its central section with a flat roof stood three storeys high and featured extensive wings, which rose two storeys. In the end, even that facility gave way to the building boom that swept downtown Calgary, and eventually the station was relegated to the hotel itself. No passenger trains pass through Calgary anymore. Tourists riding the elegant *Royal Canadian Pacific* tour train now board through a glass-covered building.

Neither the Canadian Northern nor the Grand Trunk Pacific Railways built their own stations in Calgary. The GTP moved into a former RCMP barracks, which has long vanished beneath Calgary's redevelopment. The CNo building, on the other hand, is still very much around. Built in 1905 as St. Mary's parish hall, the building was the centre of a French-Canadian section of Calgary known as Rouleauville. The area never realized its cultural potential, and in 1911 the church sold the building to the CNo. Although the railway would have preferred to build a new station when it came time to expand, its precarious wartime finances forced it to instead add a brick extension to the rear of the building.

The hall itself is a three-storey sandstone structure with a mansard roof on three sides and a Boomtown-style facade. The CNR closed the station in 1971 and it remained vacant for a number of years. Despite being gutted by a

fire, the building was restored and still stands today, but as a ballet school. Tracks still lead across a small bridge behind the building.

REGINA'S UNION STATION

It may have, on occasion, been a gamble to ride the rails in the early days on the prairies, but today that has literally become the case in Regina, with its sequence of different stations. When the CPR arrived in 1886, the first station it erected was the same standard plan, the wooden two-storey style, that it erected everywhere. It replaced that one with an Edward Colonna–designed low brick-and-stone building with a prominent tower above it. Finally,

Regina's Union station is the third building to serve as a station in Regina. Following its closure, it became a popular casino.

in 1911, in conjunction with the Canadian Northern Railway, which was busily adding branch lines, the CPR built the city's third station. In 1912 the three storey limestone building opened to traffic. The arched entrance led to a full three-storey waiting room replete with chandeliers. The station incorporated bas relief pilasters, lacy iron canopies, and carved stonework. Single-storey wings extended to each side, and the current front portion was added in 1931 as an extension to the waiting room.

To make way for this new Union Station, the earlier structure, minus tower, was moved to Broadview, Saskatchewan, where it yet stands, although in some disrepair. With the end of VIA Rail's passenger service in 1990, thanks to cutbacks in service by the government of Brian Mulroney, the station closed. Protected by the federal HRSPA, the station survived and in 1996 opened its doors as the Casino Regina. While slot machines now clatter away on the ground level, in the basement there remains a jail cell formerly used by the CN police (it now houses historic photos of Regina).

In the eastern wing, the names of the restaurants reflect the building's rail heritage: the Last Spike, the Rail Car, and the CPR lounge. The Rail Car restaurant does indeed occupy a CN passenger coach, beside which stands a CPR steam locomotive. The grand foyer still looms three storeys high, and its historic chandeliers yet dangle.

The Canadian Northern's Divisional Stations

ATHABASCA, ALBERTA

Here, the CNo's standard class-2 (plan 100-39) divisional station remains in the same spot as when it was built in 1912 and Athabasca was at that time the end of steel. It

closed in 1973 and became a seniors drop-in centre. In 2010 the Athabasca Heritage society leased the building from the town and is currently working to restore it to a 1912 appearance.

BIG VALLEY, ALBERTA

The town of Big Valley presents one the Prairies' more complete railway heritage landscapes. Built in 1912 as a class-2 divisional station by the CNo, the station reflects plan 100-39 (the same used for Athabasca's station), another of Pratt's designs. With the CNo's typical pyramid roof in the centre, the main portion is flanked by a pair of extensions, each with a small gable. As a divisional point, the station grounds also featured a roundhouse, the ruins of which still survive, and an elevator and passenger coach round out the landscape. The station, in original condition, is a station stop for the Stettler steam excursion trains, and it houses a museum inside.

CANORA, SASKATCHEWAN

The CNo station in Canora is unique in that, while it is a museum, it is still used by train passengers travelling on VIA Rail's popular Churchill train. It was built on the CNo's main Winnipeg to Edmonton line in 1904. As such, it is described as the oldest train station of this type still operating in Saskatchewan. Style-wise, it was built as a standard CNo class 3 station, but its demands as a divisional station meant that it was given an extended freight shed. It remains proudly at the head of the main street, which contains a large number of historic buildings. As a railway museum, it displays CN and pioneer artifacts.

CARMAN, MANITOBA

The CNo station in this southern Manitoba community is categorized as a class 2 station. Larger than the rural stations, it presents wings on each side of the main building, each with a hip dormer. The wing to the west contained the waiting room, while that to the east was the freight room. It was built in 1902 and is today owned by the town of Carman. It was designated in 2003 as a Manitoba Municipal Heritage Site.

DAUPHIN, MANITOBA

Although a "divisional" station, Dauphin's is one of Canada's finest examples of CNo station architecture. Built in 1912, and designed by the CNo's architect R.B. Pratt, the brick-and-stone structure rises three storeys to its iconic pyramid roof. Two-storey extensions extend out from the central structure, each with low-gable roofs, while further single-storey extensions abut that. Small castle-like turrets adorn the corners of the third storey of the central segment. More fine examples of stonework are found not only on the base but at the corners of the walls as well.

The size of the structure reflects the site's former importance as a major divisional point. The station was designated by the province of Manitoba in 1998 as a heritage resource and federally under the Heritage Railway Station Protection Act. It is now owned by the Town of Dauphin. Similar designs were created by the CNo in its Edmonton and Saskatoon stations, but these buildings no longer stand. A similar station, but with two pyramids, still stands in Thunder Bay, Ontario.

The CNo's grand divisional station in Dauphin, Manitoba, is a spectacular example of R.B. Pratt's design work. It is now owned by the town.

GLADSTONE, MANITOBA

William Mackenzie and Donald Mann enlarged their railway empire by buying up the failing Manitoba and Northwestern Railway. They chose Gladstone as a divisional point and in 1901 built its standard class-2 divisional station here. It displayed the pyramid roofline and extensions to each side of the two-storey portion, where a pair of dormers punctured the roofline. As a divisional station, it also contained dining facilities for travellers. The building was relocated to the north end of the town and now serves as the community museum. The CPR had arrived in 1882 when it acquired the Manitoba and Northwestern Railway line from Portage la Prairie to Minnedosa. Gladstone's station, to no-one's surprise, is no longer around.

HANNA, ALBERTA

The Hanna station, another of the CNo's prairie divisional points, was a standard class-2 building with the typical pyramid roof but also with extensions to each end of the structure. A prominent gable rests above the operator's bay, and smaller dormers appear on the roofs of the wings. The station, closed in the 1970s, has been removed from its original location and now serves as a tourist information office near the west entrance to the community, from Highway 9. A rare historic roundhouse still survives, awaiting proposals for its preservation.

HUMBOLDT, SASKATCHEWAN

Sensibly designated as protected in 1992, under the HRSPA, the Canadian Northern station in Humboldt dates back to 1905. Along with its pyramid roof, more typical of the CNo's rural class 3 stations, the station also features added wings to each end to accommodate extra passenger and freight traffic in this then-growing town. The CN vacated the structure prior to 2010 to move into newer facilities nearby. By late 2011, the building was empty and its streetside yard heavily overgrown, but the town of Humboldt is investigating alternative uses. The rail yards, however, remain very much is use, and yet contain a steel water tower.

KIPLING, SASKATCHEWAN

Built in 1909, the Kipling station is one of the class-2 divisional stations designed by the CNo's early architect, R.B. Pratt. Larger than his standard rural station style, it contains wings on each side of the centre portion, each with a hip gable dormer above. The centre portion reflects the railway's more typical pyramid roof, with prominent gables both front and back. Still in its original location, although turned around, the station was designated as a municipal heritage property and is now an attractive bed and breakfast.

NEEPAWA, MANITOBA

Known to its early Cree inhabitants, *Neepawa* was, in their language, the "land of plenty." The town's growth dates from the arrival of the Canadian Northern Railway in 1902, when it chose this location for a divisional point and constructed one of its standard class-2 stations for such a busy spot. With its two-storey central portion topped off by the usual pyramid roof, wings extend to the sides, each displaying the hip-gable dormers of that style. The Beautiful Plains Museum moved into the vacant building in 1981, and the station still rests on its original site, although the tracks are now gone.

RADVILLE, SASKATCHEWAN

Built in 1912 by the Canadian Northern Railway to replace a temporary boxcar station, the Radville station was constructed according to that line's plan 100-39, or class-2 style, and was one of only five such structures in Saskatchewan. It is typified by the CNo's usual pyramid roof with extensions on each side of the main section. While the centre portion rises two full storeys and has a prominent gable above the operator's bay window, the two wings have peaked dormers in the roofline. This is a divisional station on the CNo's Brandon to Lethbridge route, and the building still occupies its original site.

With the switch from steam to diesel, the round-house was closed in 1960 and demolished soon after. In 1978 the last station agent retired and the station closed.

Trains continued to use the grain elevators until the 1990s, but they, too, are now gone.

The Radville station, however, has survived and was designated as a heritage property in 1984. Still dominating the head of the main street today, it has become a museum. That main street also contains other heritage buildings, including an original hotel, formerly known as the Empire Hotel and now the Red Creek Saloon. Across from the saloon, the CIBC building was built as the Canadian Bank of Commerce in 1912, and it, too, is a designated heritage structure.

The CNo station and the grain elevators at Meeting Creek, Alberta, reflect a true prairie railway landscape.

STETTLER, ALBERTA

Built in 1911, this standard CNo 2nd-class divisional station, with its pyramid roof and extensions to both sides, now resides in the town's Town and Country Museum, where various other heritage buildings have joined it. The original site of the station is now occupied by a more modern station, which serves as the boarding point for the popular Alberta Prairie Railway steam excursions.

VERMILION, ALBERTA

Located on the main line of the CNo, which built through this area in 1905, the railway chose Vermilion as a divisional point, and a roundhouse, water tank, and grain elevators were built. The standard 2nd-class divisional station rounded out the townscape. When the CNR decided to construct a new station, the old CNo building was moved a few kilometres west to Vermilion Provincial Park. The CNR maintains a busy yard at this location, having replaced the station with a smaller, more modern flat-roofed structure constructed of brick, with a dark trim around the roofline.

The Canadian Northern's Country Stations

ASHERN, MANITOBA

Now serving as the museum office, the Canadian Northern's simple single storey station in Ashern, labelled as plan 100-68, is the focus of a pioneer village. This includes a one-room schoolhouse, a 1912 Anglican church, a one-time post office, and a pioneer log cabin. The station was built shortly after 1910, when the CNo pushed its line north to Steep Rock and Gypsumville.

AVONLEA, SASKATCHEWAN

This history-conscious community south of Regina purchased its Canadian Northern station in 1981 and converted it to the Heritage House Museum. The CNo built this class-3 station, according to its common 100-29 plan, in 1912 on its Radville to Moose Jaw line. Increased traffic in 1917 prompted the railway to extend the freight shed, and the CNR later added its typical stucco finish to the exterior. It still rests on site, virtually unaltered both outside and in, and it displays the typical kitchen, living quarters, and waiting room of the station, as well as sports and law enforcement displays. The structure was one of the hundreds of rural stations erected by the Canadian Northern Railway that were dominated by the iconic pyramid roof.

BAILDON, SASKATCHEWAN

Situated in the unusual Sukanen Ship Pioneer Village Museum, the CNo's 1911 Baildon station, one of that company's standard rural stations, has found a new home along with the McCabe grain elevator and, as with a great many such museums, a caboose. More than three dozen heritage buildings line the streets of this heritage village.

The focus of the village, however, is Tom Sukanen's "ship" — a vessel that he built in the prairie town of Macrorie, Saskatchewan, in the hopes that it would carry him, a homesick Finn, back to his homeland. During the difficult depression years, he brought in steel and wood and began to build the boat he would call the *Sontiainen*. Sadly, the ship was vandalized, and Sukanen ended up in a hospital in Battleford, where he died in 1943. For years, the remains of the vessel lay hidden in a nearby barn. Then, in 1975, thanks to a vigorous fund-raising drive, the vessel was moved to the Pioneer Village Museum south of Moose Jaw, where it was restored. In the end, the remains of the "crazy Finn" were re-interred next his beloved *Sontiainen*.

BALDUR, MANITOBA

Although it is lumped in here with the Canadian Northern stations, the Baldur station may be the only surviving example of a U.S. "northern plains" style station. There was no attempt at aesthetic or architectural embellishment: the wooden building offers only a gable roof and operator's bay. No living quarters were here. The structure was built by the Northern Pacific and Manitoba Railway (NPM) in 1890 on a line initiated by the government of Manitoba, with the intention of combating the CPR's unpopular monopoly on rail routes and grain prices. The strategy worked, and the federal government bought out the monopoly. But the NPM could not make much of a profit and sold the line to the upstart Canadian Northern Railway in 1900, thus launching that line on its way to becoming one of Canada's major railway empires. As the station was built prior to the arrival of electricity, the brackets for the kerosene lamps remain visible in the building.

The station was moved to the Manitoba Agricultural Museum a short distance south of Austin, Manitoba, in 1975. The Homesteader's Village contains twenty buildings, some of them replicas, that represent early settlement in Manitoba. Among them are the railway water tower from MacGregor, built in 1900, as well as a 1905–grain elevator from Austin. The village also contains a number of pioneer log buildings.

BELLIS, ALBERTA

Using a standard Canadian Northern 3rd-class design, this station was built by the CNR in 1923 after it had assumed the operations of the bankrupt CNo. Relocated from the village of Bellis, the station is part of the Ukrainian Heritage Village, east of Edmonton. The interior has been restored to its 1950s appearance, complete with operating equipment and agent's family accommodation on the second floor. A track runs in front of the station to a grain elevator a short distance away, thus recreating an early typical prairie railway landscape.

BLAINE LAKE, SASKATCHEWAN

Built in 1912 on the CNo's Prince Albert to North Battleford line, the station was a class 3 station, plan 100-29. The CNR ended operations in 1973 and sold the structure to the town, which now operates it as the Blaine Lake Museum. It is a municipal heritage structure and is listed on the Saskatchewan Register of Heritage Properties.

BOWSMAN, MANITOBA

Here, in the Swan Valley Historic Museum, among an extensive collection of early area buildings, is the Canadian Northern Railway's Bowsman station, built in 1900 prior to the arrival of the CNo's new architect, Ralph Benjamin Pratt. The structure is a design from the CNo's predecessor line, the Manitoba Railway, and consists of long hip gable roof with a peak gable dormer above the operator's bay window. It was one of the last built by the CNo in this style prior to Pratt's trademark pyramid-style stations. A bunk car rests on the grounds beside it, and a trapper's cabin, shingle mill, and examples of pioneer tools are also on display here. Many of the surviving stations on the Gladstone to Swan River line were built by the Manitoba Railway before it was acquired by the CNo in 1901.

CARLYLE, SASKATCHEWAN

Located in a 1910 CNo 3rd-class station, the Rusty Relics Museum has an operational telegraph key on display. Nearby are a CPR jigger and a CNR tool shed. The station is an extended version of the usual class-3 rural station. The CNR line between Maryfield and Lampman is still in use.

CEREAL, ALBERTA

This typical Canadian Northern class-3 station in Cereal, Alberta, was built by the CNo in 1911 on its Saskatoon to Calgary line. Relocated from its original site, it has been moved to another section of town and is now the Cereal Prairie Pioneer Museum.

CAMROSE, ALBERTA

The station in Camrose was one of a string built by the CNo in 1911 along its new line between that town and Stettler. Almost identical the other country stations, the Camrose station — experiencing increased traffic as the community grew — also features a more extensive freight and baggage wing.

In 1937 the CNR covered the wood-shingle siding, another typical feature of CNo stations, with stucco to provide more protection against the elements. This station is preserved as the centrepiece of Camrose Railway Park and houses the Canadian Northern Society library and archives, as well as a popular tea room. It was moved off its original site and placed on a more secure concrete foundation a short distance away. The CNo Society is responsible for helping to preserve much of central Alberta's railway heritage, overseeing sites at Big Valley, Donalda, and Meeting Creek. The Morgan Garden Railway adjacent to the station contains a miniature railway and miniature replicas of local heritage buildings.

DONALDA, ALBERTA

Although it sports the name "Donalda," this museum is in fact a fine example of a Canadian Northern 4th-class station from Vardura, Saskatchewan. It was built in 1909

according to CNo plan 100-29. Following the removal of Donalda's own station, in 1991 the Canadian Northern Society moved the building to Donalda, where the society undertook a restoration. This single-storey structure with a simple roof with gable ends contains the operator's office at one end and the freight shed at the other. Its wood-frame exterior is painted in the more traditional Tuscan red.

A historic Canadian Bank of Commerce, built in either 1928 or 1932, houses the Donalda Art Gallery. The site also contains a historic creamery.

EDAM, SASKATCHEWAN

This small village still offers a genuine railway landscape, and its rural Canadian Northern Station faces a grain elevator that contains the displays of the Harry S. Washbrook Museum. The rails, however, are gone.

The CNo built the station in 1912 to its 3rd-class plan 100-12. It operated until 1979, when the CNR closed the station. Two years later, the municipality acquired the structure, making some interior alterations, although the exterior retains much of its original appearance. Since then, the Lions Club, a play school, and a community centre have occupied the building.

FISHER BRANCH, MANITOBA

The station in Fisher Branch is another of the hundreds of rural CNo stations. It was built in 1915, closed in 1980, and is now the Rolling Memories Museum and a designated Manitoba Municipal Heritage Site. The structure has been modified slightly from its original appearance and is no longer near the tracks.

FORT SASKATCHEWAN, ALBERTA

Founded as an RCMP outpost in 1875, the village remained a hub for the area's Metis and First Nations people. Then, in 1905, the Canadian Northern Railway built its Edmonton line through the town, and Fort Saskatchewan boomed into a busy grain distribution centre containing an elevator and stockyard.

While displaying the typical CNo pyramid roof, the station is larger than most of its later counterparts and contains extended bellcast wings, a feature found on only a few other CNo stations, such as Humboldt and North Battleford in Saskatchewan. Known as CNo plan 100-19, it is the last of its kind in Alberta and is listed on the Alberta Registry of Historic Places. It has been out of service since the 1980s, and the building now serves as a museum.

GRAVELBOURG, SASKATCHEWAN

When the CNo passed through southern Saskatchewan in 1913, it added a class-3 station in this established Francophone community, which had been founded years earlier by a Quebec priest who had led a party of Franco-Americans from New York state. After the station opened, the CNo provided twice-weekly passenger service until the 1950s.

When harvests failed during the drought-stricken thirties, the CNR brought relief supplies to the community, and when grain harvests were bountiful, it brought it trainloads of harvesters on what were known as the "Harvester specials."

From 1987 until 1997, the station served as the town office. Today, it stands at its original site, although turned around, and is now a residence. In 1987 the branch was absorbed into the CPR system, which still operates the line and hauls grain from the town's two remaining elevators.

GILBERT PLAINS, MANITOBA

One station that employed a less-common style is the CNo station in Gilbert Plains. Built in 1900, it offers hip

gables at each end with a peak gable above the operator's bay window. It is now a seniors drop-in centre at Main and Gordon Streets, close to its original location.

An identical station, originally built in Bowsman, is now at the Swan Valley Museum in Swan River. As with the CNo Winnipegosis station, this style predated Pratt's arrival.

LANGHAM, SASKATCHEWAN

This former CNo 3rd-class, plan 100-39 station in Langham, built in 1905, became the community's museum in 2001 and is situated close to its original location on Railway Street. The freight shed is an extended version of the standard shed. Shared with the Wheatland Library, the displays include household artifacts and the "flour sack story": what the ingenious pioneers were able to create using simple flour sacks.

LUNDAR, MANITOBA

Still on its original site, although turned around now, the Lundar station is another of those typical CNo class-3 stations. Located north of Winnipeg on the branch line that led to Gypsumville, the building is now, like so many others, a museum. This heritage village offers visitors the Mary Hill School, the Notre Dame church, two log houses, and an Icelandic library. The focus is, of course, the railway, and the grounds include the former CNo railway station as well as the usual caboose

MAIDSTONE, SASKATCHEWAN

This rural CNo class-3 station with an extended freight shed was relocated in 1990 to 2nd Street, where it is the focus of the Maidstone and District museum, along with the usual caboose and other heritage buildings, such as a barber shop, store, and church. It was built in

1905 on the CNo's main line between North Battleford and Lloydminister and operated until passenger service ended in 1977. In 1989 the Province of Saskatchewan designated it as a heritage property.

MCCONNELL, MANITOBA

This standard CNo class-3 rural station was built in McConnell on the Beulah Halboro branch in 1909. Following its closure, it was heavily vandalized until it was rescued by the town of Hamiota and moved to the Hamiota Pioneer Club Museum grounds on 7th Street. A historic church has been moved from Oakner to the grounds as well. The abandoned rail line has become a recreational trail.

MCCREARY, MANITOBA

This is another typical Canadian Northern small town station, built in 1912 on the Dauphin to The Pas line, according to plan 100-29. It retains many of those original features, including the steep pyramid roof devised by R.B. Pratt and a grey-stucco exterior applied in the 1930s by the CNR. The railway closed the building in 1980s, and in 1991 the province designated it as a provincial heritage property. The town purchased the building in 1997 to develop it as a museum

MEETING CREEK, ALBERTA

This community is another example of a genuine surviving prairie heritage railway landscape. With its nearby grain elevators, the village of Meeting Creek presents a true vestige of the Prairies' railway heritage. The station was built by the Canadian Northern Railway in its class-3 rural style. In 1911, urged on by Premier Alexander Rutherford, the CNo extended its tracks between Camrose and Stettler, bypassing the original settlement of Meeting

Creek by eight kilometres. As was usually the case, the village moved closer to the station. The first train to reach town was greeted by the local band

Although the station fell silent in the 1960s, it remained standing and in 1988 was converted by the Canadian Northern Society to an interpretative centre and restored to resemble its 1950s appearance. A small wooden trestle still exists a short distance west of the station and grain elevators.

In 1997 the branch line's owner, the Central Western Railway, abandoned the line, but in so doing donated enough trackage to ensure the preservation of this genuine prairie railway landscape.

MIAMI, MANITOBA

The structure in this southern Manitoba community predates many of the surviving stations in this province. In fact, it was built as early as 1889 by the Northern Pacific and Manitoba Railway Company (NP&M) and shortly thereafter acquired by William Mackenzie and Donald Mann to help launch that duo's monumental railway empire.

The station is the sole survivor of three built in this rare style by the Northern Pacific and Manitoba Railway in 1889. Before the arrival of the Canadian Northern Railway, the NP&M was one of the first railways to challenge the CPR's dominance in western Manitoba. The unusual two-storey building sports hip end gables and an observation bay on the second floor, directly above the operator's ground floor bay window. It is the only surviving station with such a feature.

Moved slightly from its original foundation, the Miami station was designated as a municipal heritage structure in 2008 and today houses a museum.

MOOSEHORN, MANITOBA

The simple single-storey CNo station, built to one of that line's 4th-class plans (plan 100-68) now rests next to the Moosehorn Heritage Museum, which is housed in a historic Masonic Hall. The agent's quarters were located at the rear of the building instead of the second floor.

NORQUAY, SASKATCHEWAN

Situated northeast of Yorkton near the Manitoba border, the village of Norquay sprang to life when the CNo arrived in 1911 and constructed one of its standard rural class-3 stations. Settlers, including ranchers and lumber men, had begun arriving earlier when the CPR reached Yorkton in 1898. Located close to its original site, the building is now the Whistle Stop Restaurant.

PRAIRIE RIVER, ALBERTA

Now a museum, the Prairie River CNo station was designated as a municipal heritage property in 1982 and since 1985 has served as the Prairie River Museum. The collection displays artifacts depicting pioneer and aboriginal life in the area, as well as a railway saw mill and planer, which operated until 1917.

Wadena's CNo class 3 station is now a museum.

The CNo erected this station in 1919 even as the company's corporate health was failing. In fact, the building was transferred to the Canadian National Railway (CNR) later that year. The station was listed as CNo plan 100-72, a common later design for 3rd-class stations used in small communities across the province. The station is listed on the Saskatchewan Register of Heritage Properties.

ROBLIN, MANITOBA

In 1906 the CNo built one of their standard 3rd-class stations to plan 100-3 in this community. On the main line from Winnipeg to Edmonton, the extra business in the area required a longer than normal freight shed.

The station closed in 1978 and is now a popular Austrian restaurant known as the Station Café. In addition to serving food, the restaurant has replicated the agent's office and displays railway memorabilia. Its exterior has been little-altered, save for a paint job. It remains on its original site, although no yard buildings remain.

ROWLEY, ALBERTA

This CNo 3rd-class station helps to form another one of the Prairies' better railway heritage landscapes. Not only does the structure remain on site, it has been preserved as a station. One of the last of the plan 100-72 CNo stations, it was built in 1922 on the Stettler subdivision. Rowley is also a ghost town attraction, and, because it has attracted filmmakers, it is nicknamed "Rowleywood."

ST. JAMES, MANITOBA

This single-storey structure was built in 1910 by the Canadian Northern Railway at the west end of Winnipeg and was part of the line's Oak Point Subdivision. The structure is a CNo 4th-class single-storey rural station.

In 1974 the Winnipeg's Vintage Locomotive Society acquired the historic building to use as their boarding point for the popular Prairie Dog Central Railway steam and diesel excursions. With the abandonment of the subdivision by the CN in 1996, the society moved the station to a more rural location on Inkster Boulevard, where it continues to play out its important heritage role. Designated as a federally protected station, its ticket office, two waiting rooms, and freight rooms have been restored to reflect its historic train operations. The Prairie Dog Central Railway steam locomotive can often be seen puffing impatiently in front.

ST. WALBURG, SASKATCHEWAN

Although constructed by CNR in 1922, this 4th-class design was first introduced by the Canadian Northern Railway in 1907 as plan 100-68. The CNR modified the design somewhat after assuming control of the CNo. According to the Saskatchewan Resister of Heritage Properties, it was one of over seventy stations of this basic style constructed in Ontario, Manitoba, Saskatchewan, Alberta, and Minnesota. It lacked second-storey living accommodations.

The building is now used as an interpretative centre.

SHELLBROOK, SASKATCHEWAN

Settlers began arriving into the Shellbrook area as early as 1882. Even by 1905, there was little more than a general store and post office. In 1909 the CNo laid out the townsite and built one of their standard class-3, plan 100-29 country stations. As business improved, the freight shed was extended, and later, in the 1930s, the CNR applied a coating of stucco to the exterior. The first train of the CNo arrived in January of 1910.

The station has become a museum, and happily it remains on site at the foot of the main street, where it faces a small "elevator row."

SMOKEY LAKE, ALBERTA

In 1919, as one of the Canadian Northern Railway's last acts of railway building, it extended a line from Edmonton in a northeasterly direction in order to open settlement lands for returning First World War veterans. Known as plan 100-72, a slightly larger version of the CNo's 3rd-class stations, the station in Smokey Lake is nonetheless nearly identical in appearance to the hundreds of other CNo stations erected across the prairies, and like those others it owes its design to R.B. Pratt.

In 1936 the new owners, the CNR, covered the wood-shingle siding with stucco and repainted the station in its standard green-and-yellow paint scheme. Following the closing of the station and the removal of the tracks, the building was moved a few metres back from the now vacant right of way, while a caboose rests on a section of track nearby. The right of way now forms part of the Iron Horse rail trail.

STURGIS, SASKATCHEWAN

In 1911, when the tracks of the CNo finally reached Sturgis from Pelly, a box car served as the first station. When the line arrived from Canora in 1914, the railway added another of its later standard rural class-3, plan 100-72 stations, and the village became the leading cattle shipper in eastern Saskatchewan. The CNR used the structure until 1984, when the railway indicated its intention to demolish it. Worried about losing their most significant heritage structure, residents of Sturgis formed a committee of volunteers and raised funds to relocate the building a short distance away. Today, it functions as a museum and displays many elements of the history of the town and its area, including farm and household items and the obligatory caboose.

TURTLEFORD, SASKATCHEWAN

This standard class-3 CNo station, built on the North Battleford to Turtleford branch, has been relocated to become the district museum. Intended as a loop line between North Battleford and Edmonton, the route was meant to help open the territory north of the North Saskatchewan River to settlers. The Saskatchewan end of the line reached Turtleford from North Battleford in 1914, but the demands of the First World War suspended the work. By the time construction resumed in 1919, the CNo was no more. The CNR, which had assumed control of the CNo, managed to extend track from Turtleford to St. Walburg in 1921, but the western section was halted at Heinsburg in 1928. The vital gap was never filled.

WADENA, SASKATCHEWAN

This 3rd-class CNo station, the most common style on the prairies, was built by John Skoglund in 1904, and passenger service began the following April. When the CPR built its line across the tracks of the CNo, the station was moved twenty-five metres to the east.

The CNR halted passenger service in 1963 and by 1981 had closed this station. In that year, the municipality purchased the building and moved it to the south end of the village, where it is now the focus of the town's heritage village. The site includes rail artifacts such as a hand car, crossing signals, a telegraph wire, and the omnipresent caboose. The grounds also contain a Mountie barracks, a 1914 homestead, and a historic school house. Wadena's CPR station is also well-preserved and is now a private home west of the community

WALDHEIM, SASKATCHEWAN

Although Mennonite settlers had begun arriving as early as 1893, the CNo did not lay tracks here until

1909, when it erected its typical rural class-3 station on its Carlton Subdivision north of Saskatoon. Still on its original location, the town acquired the building in 1983 and it now houses a library and museum.

WINNIPEGOSIS, MANITOBA

Before the CNo lured station architect Ralph Benjamin Pratt away from the CPR, the CNo's earlier stations in Manitoba offered a different appearance. Hip gables marked the front and rear, a two-storey roof over the operator's bay window. In the Winnipegosis station, a pair of extensions stretch from each side of the ticket office, one housing a waiting room and the other, the freight room. Each extension sports similar hip gables on the ends of its two wings. Similar structures also stood in Manitoba at Swan River, Ochre River, and Ethelbert.

Built in 1897, this large station is now the home of the Winnipegosis Museum, a project of the Winnipegosis Historical Society. The grounds also contain the vessel *Myrtle M.*, built in 1938 to serve the Lake Winnipegosis fishing industry.

The GTP Survivors

As with the CNo, the Grand Trunk Pacific used only a limited range of railway station patterns. While the country stations varied slightly in the shape of the gable and bay, the original divisional stations generally copied the same styles used by its sister rail line, the National Transcontinental Railway, east of Winnipeg. These were large two-storey structures, some of which held a prominent gable midway along the roofline, while others had cross gables at each end of the roof. A few were half-timbered to reflect a tudoresque flair. The only survivor

of this style is at Melville, Saskatchewan, and replacement division stations built by the CNR were simpler in style. The GTP built only one main line across the prairies and few branch lines. As a result, few stations remain, since few were ever built.

DIVISIONAL STATIONS
Biggar, Saskatchewan

This view of the Biggar station shows that even federal designation cannot save a station from neglect.

In February 1996, Sheila Copps, federal minister of heritage, arrived in Biggar to declare its historic GTP station "protected" under the Historical Railway Station Protection Act.

At the time it opened in 1910, the GTP station in Biggar was considered the largest GTP station in the west. The building displays a simple elegance, with a steep bellcast roof and prominent gable above the operator's bay window.

In 1986 the dispatching system was automated and passenger service ended. In that year, the station closed. With five hundred railway workers and the confluence of three GTP lines as well as a CPR line, the town was totally railway dependant. In many ways it still is. A new CN bunkhouse was built for the 150 CN employees and stands opposite the "protected" station.

Regrettably, that heritage building is suffering from demolition by neglect. Following its new designation, it remained unused and rotting. By late 2011, portions of the overhang were falling off, while large bushes pushed through the cracks in its foundation.

Melville, Saskatchewan

When the GTP designed its divisional stations, it opted for a large structure. Melville's station, built in 1908, was one of a handful of such designs on the GTP/NTR line and was built by Carter Hall and Adlinger. The original divisional station in Rivers, Manitoba was identical to this style, as is the one still standing in Sioux Lookout, Ontario.

The GTP's grand Melville divisional station is in the early stages of restoration.

The building is a full two storeys with half-timbered gables on the roof over the operator's bay, and another gable at the end, as well as another set on the town side. As with most divisional stations, that in Melville contained a restaurant, which was known as the Beanery. Proposals for its reuse have included converting it to a Western Hockey Hall of Fame. Throughout 2011, volunteers were hard at work cleaning up the interior. As is typical in a prairie town, the building dominates the foot of the main street. A GTP station imported from Duff now sits in the Melville Regional Park, along with a steam engine (see museums).

Rivers, Manitoba

In 1908, as the GTP main line proceeded across the prairies, the company chose Rivers as a divisional point and here built a station using the same overall plan as that found at Melville. As was its practice, the GTP named the station after one of its own: President Sir Charles Rivers-Wilson. A full two storeys, the station displayed the two cross gables at the ends of the building and a bay window at the east end. The yards contained a roundhouse, a repair shop, and coal shed. In 1917 the GTP replaced it with a new storey-and-a-half station with a wide bellcast roof and half-timbered, stucco-covered gables on both the track and street sides. But, with the advent of diesel, the steam facilities were no longer needed, and all structures associated with the station's divisional role — the water tower, the roundhouse, and the bunkhouse — were removed. Only a few sidings remain in the once busy yards.

Today, the solid-brick station, although federally designated as a protected heritage station, is vacant and falling into disrepair, but it is not as seriously damaged as in the station in Biggar, and a local community is working to restore it. VIA passengers now use a small shelter transported to the location from North Brandon.

THE COUNTRY STATIONS

Delburne, Alberta

This central Alberta Community has preserved its standard-plan Grand Trunk Pacific station as well as its wooden water tower. The tower contains four levels of displays, including a replica coal mine and a school room, all on the grounds of the Anthony Henday Museum. This station varies from other GTP country stations in that the operator's bay window and the dormer immediately above it, the agent's apartment, are octagonal in shape. Also on the grounds is a CN caboose.

Edgerton, Alberta

Here on the grounds of the Edgerton and District Museum, the 1909 GTP station (plan 100-152), relocated from its original site, houses a rare collection of autochrome photographs taken by Hugo Viewager between 1913 and 1914. The grounds also include the Battle Valley and Edgerton Methodist Church, as well as a display of older autos and tractors. The station is located at Highways 894 and 610.

Edson, Alberta

Edson sprang into existence when the GTP extended its line west of Edmonton in 1911 and named the location after Edson Chamberlain, the line's general manager. The Edson station also marked the location of the Alberta Coal Branch, as well as being a jumping-off point for settlers en route to their homesteads in the Grande Prairie region. Representing a simpler version of the standard-plan stations, plan 100-153, this station had its roof modified when it was moved to Centennial Park in 1975. Now named the Galloway Station Museum, its displays include railway and coal-mining artifacts. Funding from three levels of government helped upgrade the museum, which held its grand opening on September 25, 2011.

The Museum is operated by the Edson and District Historical Society.

Evansburg, Alberta

Tipple Park is appropriately named, as the town of Evansburg was one of Alberta's earliest coal mining towns. It dates to 1907, when coal was first extracted, but the lack of a railway hindered economic shipments. At first, as the Grand Trunk Pacific Railway built its tracks west from Edmonton in 1909, it ended its tracks at Entwhistle on the east side of the Pembina River opposite Evansburg. The gorge was too difficult to quickly bridge, and it would take until 1912 before one was complete. As a result, the two communities boomed. Although the stations from both towns no longer stand, that from MacLeod River was moved to Tipple Park, where it is now the heritage centerpiece … along with a caboose. It is a standard-plan GTP single-storey small town station with an octagonal dormer and bay window.

Fort Qu'Appelle, Saskatchewan

Located at the convergence of several early trails, the site attracted a Hudson's Bay trading, an RCMP fort, and a mission. The trading post, dating from 1897, still stands. Its railway story would have had more significance had the CPR followed through with its original plan to construct its main line across the valley in this location. Instead, the CPR opted for Regina — a less attractive location but one where flatter terrain meant lower costs.

In 1911 the GTP reached Fort Qu'Appelle with a line connecting Melville with Regina and Northgate on the North Dakota border. It was one of only a few branch lines constructed by the GTP. The railway built an extended version of its standard plan 100-152 rural station with the polygonal dormer rising above the bay window. Unlike others of this plan, the bay and the dormer lie in the centre of the structure. Still on its original site, the station closed in 1962 and is now a tourist information office.

Nokomis, Saskatchewan

The Grand Trunk Pacific, on what began as the Qu'Appelle, Long Lake and Saskatchewan line, built a station identical to the CPR's standard plan #10 pattern. The building was moved to the present site on Highway 5 in 1977, where, along with a caboose, it is the focus of the Nokomis and District Museum.

Portage la Prairie, Manitoba, CN/VIA

This sturdy station was built by the Grand Trunk Pacific Railway in 1908 on its main line from Winnipeg to Saskatoon. Originally a "union" station serving both the GTP and the Great Northern Railway of Manitoba, it was built in a style different from most of its GTP contemporaries. In fact, it may well have been influenced by the GNR. It is a long, single-storey brick building with a low, wide-flared roofline and a pair of gables on both the track and street side, including one above the operator's bay and one over the entrance. The station is still in railway use and a is stop for VIA Rail on both its transcontinental and Churchill trains, as well as for interurban buses; it lies only a few metres from the equally historic CPR station. The CNo also built a station nearby, but it burned down in 1960.

Three Hills, Alberta

Now the focus of the Kneehill and District Museum in Three Hills, this GTP station may have been one of the last built by that failing line. Dating from 1919, it displays a square dormer above the operator's bay and an unusual recessed dormer at the end. This was the railway's plan 100-151, one of only a dozen built in the prairies. These dormers reflect the agent's living quarters. A caboose sits in front of the station.

Viking, Alberta

The Grand Trunk Pacific station was built in 1911 to the GTP's plan 100-154. The roofline includes square dormers, both at the end and above the operator's bay, which too was square. It remains near its original site in and is now known as the Viking Station Gallery and Art Centre. It is located on 51st Street. The location is also a flag stop for VIA Rail's transcontinental train, *The Canadian*.

The CNR Survivors

When the CNR assumed operations of the Canadian Northern and Grand Trunk Pacific railways, they initially used existing stations. Once the CNR began to extend its own branch lines, it adopted a distinctive style for its rural stations: a boxy, two-storey structure with little embellishment. Its divisional stations, however, tended to demonstrate more flair and imagination.

The CNR, through the 1920s, took on the ambitious task of completing the on-again off-again line to Churchill on Hudson's Bay; prairie farmers had long lobbied for their own access to a prairie grain port. While that line does not traverse the usual prairie grasslands and wheat fields, this connection to the Prairies' economy and culture brings it and its railway features into the fold of Canada's prairie railway heritage.

DIVISIONAL STATIONS

North Battleford, Saskatchewan

Battleford, Saskatchewan, is one of the province's most historic sites. Here, Fort Battleford was built to house the North-West Mounted Police to help keep the peace in this troubled area. In 1876 it was designated as the territorial capital. After it lost that role to Regina in 1883, a depression set in until the CNo indicated that it was forging its main line along the banks of the North Saskatchewan. But then depression returned when the residents learned that this new railway divisional point would be on the opposite side of the river and would be of no use to them at all.

The GTP eventually did bring a line through old Battleford, but it was too little, too late, and the station was little more than their typical country depot. The GTP linked with CNo north of the community at Battleford Junction. When the CNR assumed both lines, it removed the former GTP portion. Today, of course, the two communities are completely linked and are known as "The Battlefords." Government House still stands and it, along with the fort, are national historic sites.

The solid brick station in this historic community is another one of the few constructed by the Canadian National Railways during the 1950s. The style is known as the International style and consists of a flat roofline and modernistic raised aluminum lettering. A second floor houses staff offices for the divisional yard in front of the station. In 1995 the building was designated as a protected station under the Heritage Railway Stations Protection Act.

It replaced a standard CNo class-2 divisional-point station. That station, built in 1911, was moved to 22nd Street to become the Pennydale Junction Restaurant. Although a divisional station, it looked very much like the more typical 3rd-class stations with the pyramid roof rising above the two storey central section. It differs in that two wings extend to the sides and display wide, low, bellcast rooflines. The CNo built a few of its divisional stations to this style, such as that at Humboldt. The facade of the old station has been significantly altered.

East of the station, the Western Prairie Development Museum contains the relocated CNo 4th-class station from St. Albert, Alberta, as well as a steam locomotive with box car and caboose appended.

Prince Albert

Originally a terminus for the Qu'Appelle, Long Lake and Saskatchewan Railway (QLL&S) in 1889, this line linked the growing cities of Regina and Saskatoon with the steamers on the North Saskatchewan River, at what was then the mission village of Prince Albert. The first station, built in 1891, was a standard QLL&S wooden hip-gable style. The line was operated by the CPR until the CNo acquired the route in 1906 and built one of its standard class-2 divisional point stations. Later, the busy yards developed further when the CNo also extended its line from Hudson Bay, Manitoba, through Prince Albert to Shellbrook in 1910.

The CNo had originally intended that Prince Albert be on its main line but instead opted for a more southerly route from Gladstone in Manitoba directly to Edmonton. The CPR didn't leave town entirely, though, and it ran its trains along the CNR line from Hague. The Grand Trunk Pacific extended its line northward from Young, reaching St. Louis in 1914 and Prince Albert in 1917, and the town appeared poised to become a significant rail hub for northern Saskatchewan. Through the 1990s, both the CN and CP gave up their routes, abandoning many of their branch lines out of Prince Albert. Meanwhile, the CN line from Hague was acquired by Omnitrax as the Carlton Trail Railway (CTR) short line. The former CNR station was built in the 1950s in the modern international style as a two-storey flat-roofed structure with

raised aluminum station letters, and it now serves as a business office, while the roundhouse, built in 1959, still provides repairs for the CTR.

Vegreville, Alberta

Unlike most prairie stations, the one in Vegreville was added by the Canadian National Railway itself. After having assumed such bankrupt rail lines as the Grand Trunk Pacific and the Canadian Northern, the CNR simply opted to recycle existing station buildings. However, when the rival CPR extended a branch line through Vegreville, the CNR replaced the earlier Canadian Northern station with a larger one. Built in 1930, the new Vegreville station incorporated separate men's and women's waiting rooms as well as washrooms and then built a smoking room.

At the time, Vegreville served as a divisional point, but with the replacement of steam with diesel, that function was no longer needed and none of the divisional structures remain — although the yards still contain extensive sidings. This distinctive station offers many aesthetically pleasing features, not typical of stations being built in this period. It has a high, steep bellcast roof with a prominent half-timbered gable above the operators' bay window. A second prominent gable punctures the trackside roof, while smaller hip gable dormers also appear, representing the agent's living quarters and office facilities for the divisional employees. The station still stands in excellent condition and is now the Lakustra Heritage Foundation community museum and tea room. A separate shelter offers VIA Rail passengers a facility for the transcontinental Canadian.

Wainwright, Saskatchewan

Another of the more attractive surviving prairie stations is that which yet dominates the foot of Wainwright's main street. Once the GTP had finished bridging the Battle River with one of the province's largest wooden trestles, one that still attracts awe-struck visitors, it selected a location to its east for a divisional point. It built a station there that had a bellcast roof and prominent gables. The building burned to the ground in 1928 and the CNR, then the owner of the former GTP, put its architects to work to design a new building. The new structure was much larger and again included a wide bellcast roof with prominent gables above both the operator's bay and the street entrance. Wider and longer than the first station, the replacement building also had hip dormer windows where the second floor offices and accommodation were located.

The new station opened in 1930. In an ironic twist, a year after the first station burned, the same fate befell the entire main street, leaving only the unfinished station and one other structure standing. Following the station's closure, the Battle River Historical Society moved the museum collection into the building. True to its original function as a divisional station, the Galleria Restaurant operates in it as well. The new main street has received provincial funding for restoration and remains dominated by a large, free-standing memorial clock tower — the only main street structure to survive the 1929 fire. A separate shelter accommodates passengers waiting for VIA Rail's popular transcontinental train, *The Canadian*.

Wainwright's CNR divisional station has been converted to a community museum and restaurant.

THE COUNTRY STATIONS

Cudworth, Saskatchewan

The station built here in 1925 follows the distinctive pattern devised by the then newly formed Canadian National Railway. Known as plan 100-184, it is a full two-storeys, unlike many of the CNR's predecessor's earlier rural station plans, which were content with a simple storey-and-a-half. Unlike many surviving GTP and CNo stations, which the CNR covered with stucco, the original wood siding is exposed. The station was situated on a seventy-five-kilometre branch line built by the CNR that connected with the Young to Prince Albert line. It closed in the 1980s and now serves as the community museum.

Eatonia, Saskatchewan

The Canadian Northern Railway had not yet completed its line through Eatonia when it went bankrupt in 1918. It had already designated the location as a divisional point on its new McRorie subdivision and built the usual roundhouse and water tower. The Canadian National Railway, which had assumed control of both the Canadian Northern and Grand Trunk Pacific Railways, finished the line and built a station using a new pattern influenced by the stations on the National Transcontinental Railway, which the CNR had also assumed control of. Unlike the CNo and its preference for pyramid roofs, the CNR adopted a more functional square shape with a lower roofline, and it continued to operate a divisional point at this location. A row of four windows appears on the second floor and represents the quarters for the agent and his family. A long freight shed also extends to the west of the building.

The town purchased the station, leaving it on-site and created a heritage park around it. The park includes a caboose and what is known as a "catalogue" house — during the 1920s and 30s, many prairie residents would order their homes prefabricated through the Eaton's catalogue. These are considered heritage structures on the Prairies.

Frenchman's Butte, Saskatchewan

A later CN-style station building built in 1929, the museum in Frenchman's Butte offers a sweeping vista across the North Saskatchewan River. The museum also offers a tea house in a log cabin, a blacksmith's shop, and other heritage buildings, as well as displays of the area housed in a new Quonset hut. The style of the CN station, known as 100-253, with its full two storeys, is typical of that adopted by the CNR along its own new branch lines during that period. By 1979 the branch line was gone and the station became an interesting area museum, and it remains on its original site.

Glaslyn, Saskatchewan

This community displays a near-complete railway heritage landscape. The 1926 CNR station, with its full second storey, still rests by the railway right of way, as does the old wooden water tower. Inside the restored station are the agent's office and living quarters, while inside the water tower one still finds the engine and pump. Naturally enough, a caboose lurks nearby.

Kelvington, Saskatchewan

Even after the Canadian National Railway assumed operations of the Canadian Northern Railway, it continued for a time to employ that defunct line's standard plans. When the CNR opened a branch of its own into Kelvington in 1922, it retained a slightly extended version of the of the CNo's pyramid roof pattern, plan 100-75. The main differences are subtle and include a less-pronounced peak and an overhang that extends the entire length of the station. The station closed in 1977 and is now a municipal heritage property known as the Heritage Place Museum. It remains close to the CNR's still active track.

Moose Jaw, Saskatchewan, CNR station

Moose Jaw is fortunate to have not just one but two architecturally significant stations. While Hugh Jones used Italianate as his inspiration for the CPR station, John Schoefield, the rising young architect of the newly formed CNR, employed the "restrained" Classical Revival style, then coming into vogue for the CNR's new buildings. Built in 1919, the CNR's station was one of the first major stations constructed by the newly formed railway company, although it was not a divisional station, despite its size. It arrived too late to have any impact upon the urban form of the community, unlike the CPR station, which dominates the main commercial street and sits somewhat incongruously in a residential neighbourhood.

The two-storey buff brick structure features single storey wings projecting from each end. The flat roof, symmetrical shape, and modified ornamentation are all typical of the new rage of simpler architecture. Its few ornamental elements include pilasters, a concrete ridge below the roofline, and a slightly projecting facade. Schoefield would later go on to design such grand CNR stations as that in Edmonton (demolished) and Hamilton, Ontario (restored). As with the CPR station, this building has received protection under the HRSPA, though it has become a spa. The tracks have been removed, and that side of the building is now fenced off and overgrown.

Rabbit Lake, Saskatchewan

Settlers began trooping into this area when the CNo arrived in North Battleford in 1905. Another twenty years would pass, however, before the CNR would finally build a station in Rabbit Lake. But its heyday would not last. When the CNR pulled out, the population declined, and today Rabbit Lake has fewer than ninety residents, with many of the former businesses now empty. Now a museum, the Rabbit Lake station was constructed in the CNR's standard 3rd-class style, with a low roofline and full second storey.

Shell Lake, Saskatchewan

Built in 1930 on the now-abandoned Prince Albert to Lloydminister branch, this CNR 3rd-class station now houses the Shell Lake Museum but sits on its original site. Sold to the town of Shell Lake in 1982, the building retains many of its original features, including the stucco finish popular with the CNR. The tracks no longer exist, although, of course, a caboose does.

The Hudson Bay Railway

Completed to Churchill by the CNR in 1929, the Hudson Bay Railway contains a distinct collection of specially designed CNR stations.

HUDSON BAY, SASKATCHEWAN

While located nowhere near the water body of that name, Hudson Bay did arise along the railway, which built to that bay. The community first developed in 1905 as a CNo divisional point on the line from Dauphin to Prince Albert. In 1910 the railway built a branch to The Pas as part of its plan to complete the Hudson Bay Railway. Later, when the CNR resumed work on the Hudson Bay railway north of The Pas, Hudson Bay Junction gained increased importance. Although the CNo station was demolished, the

Al Mazur Memorial Heritage Park contains a Canadian National standard plan, two-storey station. It was originally located in Reserve, a short distance to the south, and visitors may take short rides along the tracks in front of it. The park itself is designed to resemble the former village of Hudson Bay Junction. The site also offers a variety of historic buildings and artifacts.

THE PAS, MANITOBA

Although the CNo had taken on the task of building a line to the shores of Hudson's Bay, by 1910 its line went no further than The Pas on the south bank of the Saskatchewan River. In 1913 the Canadian Government — which had resumed the construction of the Hudson Bay Railway, at that point destined for Port Nelson — bridged the Saskatchewan River and continued construction of the route as far as Kettle Rapids on the Nelson River, when the war suspended construction.

Built in 1928, The Pas station used multicoloured brick and is a storey-and-a-half in size. An unusually long structure, it sports a high bellcast roof with front gable dormers. It was designated as a federal heritage station in 1992. The Pas is the also sub-headquarters of the First Nations–run Keewatin Railway, which operates twice-weekly mixed trains along a branch of the HBR that then led to Flin Flon and Lynn Lake. The trains of the Keewatin Railway today run via Cranberry Portage to Pukatawagan, a distance of 250 kilometres.

CRANBERRY PORTAGE, MANITOBA

The CNR built what was a standard two-storey class-2 station in 1929 after it had assumed completion of the Hudson Bay Railway. The station sits on a branch line that led from the main route of the HBR to Flin Flon. Designated as federal heritage station in 1992, it was purchased in 2010 by the Cranberry Portage Heritage museum. In 1953 the CNR extended a branch line from Cranberry Portage to Lynn Lake to access the mines then opening in the region.

FLIN FLON, MANITOBA

Built by the CNR in 1934, the single-storey station boasts a low, wide bellcast roofline. It was purchased by the Chamber of Commerce in 1983 and moved to its current location to operate as a museum. The museum includes railway artifacts pertaining to the mining history of the area, such as a Plymouth locomotive, an ore car, and a maintenance of way train sweeper, which were all used by the Hudson Bay Mining and Smelting Company. Oh, and a sixty-three-pound trout.

GILLAM, MANITOBA

The Gillam station, built in 1930, dates from the completion of the Hudson Bay Railway to Churchill. The building was constructed of wood by the CNR and offers a prominent gable above the waiting room, as well as a string of four bellcast dormers over the freight wing, where the agent's quarters were situated. The building also displays a wraparound bellcast eave. As Gillam has no highway connection, the station remains vital to the community and is still in use by the Hudson Bay Railway (a division of Omnitrax) and by VIA Rail for its Churchill trains. It was designated as a federal heritage station in 1992.

THOMPSON, MANITOBA

This more modern station was built by the CNR in 1960 on a short branch line to access the mines in the area. The style is single storey with a low, sloped roofline and ample modern windows. It remains used by VIA Rail for its Churchill train.

CHURCHILL, MANITOBA

As befits a railway terminal, the Churchill station, built by the CNR in 1929, speaks of a grandeur larger than the town itself. Built in what is called the Queen Anne revival style, its most prominent feature is a high-pitch cross-gable roof peak rising above the main two-storey portion of the building. The building is a wood frame structure clad in asbestos shingle siding, with wooden banding around the base. An extensive two-storey wing with a shallower roofline contains a series of four hip gable dormers to represent staff offices and facilities. In fact, it is almost a modern Châteauesque style of architecture. Inside the building, a warm, spacious waiting room yet contains its original wooden benches. The station was designated as a federal heritage station in 1992. It is a popular destination for VIA Rail travellers wishing to view the polar bears of the area, or simply looking to enjoy a rail experience to Canada's Arctic reaches. Fort Prince of Wales is nearby and, like the ghost port of Port Nelson, can be seen from the air.

The CPR Survivors

For the most part, Canada's railways excelled at demolishing their stations almost as soon as they finished with them, and none was more proficient than the CPR, which is why so few survive. And those that have are almost invariably removed from their heritage sites.

DIVISIONAL STATIONS

Bassano, Alberta

At Bassano in 1911, the CPR built what was basically their common Western Line plan N-10 station, a full two-storey structure with a hip gable dormer. But with the selection of the location as a divisional point, the structure received large extensions at both ends of the building. At the end of 2011, it was being prepared for a move to Beiseker, where the station in that community remains on its original site, although now turned around. It now functions as a municipal office and library. A steel water tower still stands in Bassano, as do a variety of heritage buildings, including a bank and hotel along its main street.

While the rails in Beiseker are long gone, those in Bassano remain part of CPR's busy main line. The Bassano dam, which fed the Brooks Aqueduct, lies just seven kilometres away and, along with the aqueduct, it is a national historic site.

Brandon, Manitoba

Shortly after the CPR extended its new transcontinental line west from Winnipeg and replaced the steamboat and ferry service on the Assiniboine River, Brandon became a divisional point. It grew into a hub of various branch lines with the Grand Trunk Pacific and the Canadian Northern also converging on the emerging community. By 1912 one estimate suggests that there were more than three hundred passenger trains and nearly five hundred freight trains reaching Brandon every week.

Not too surprisingly, soon the original station was badly outdated. By 1900 the CPR had replaced the aging wooden building with a much grander edifice. In 1911, as Brandon continued to grow, the CPR replaced it with one of its more distinctive prairie stations. The most prominent feature of this newer station is its street-side facade, for this was the railway's face for the community. Two storeys in height, the main entrance is centred between two pilasters and is topped by a full entablature and a stepped parapet, which contains a clock and date stone. The exterior includes brick, stone, and etched cement designed to resemble marble. In many ways, it is designed to resemble a miniature big-city station. This federally designated heritage building now houses private businesses.

Broadview, Saskatchewan

The Romanesque Broadview station was moved to this location by the CPR in 1913 to replace its outdated Van Horne–style wooden depot. The newly arrived station had until then been the CPR station in Regina, where it also boasted a prominent tower. As the Broadview location was also a divisional point on the railway's transcontinental line, a restaurant was added beside it. The attractive building is constructed of red brick on top of a stone base, and it displays rounded windows typical of the Romanesque style. A prominent gable rests above the trackside entrance. Although it is a designated heritage station, by 2011 it remained in a state of neglect.

Opening its doors in 1972, the pioneer village museum in Broadview, Saskatchewan, offers, among the many pioneer buildings and displays, the CPR portable-style station from the community of Percival. As is often the case, a caboose is open for inspection.

Coutts, Alberta

Unusual in both form and function, the Coutts station was a lunch stop and customs station that straddled the border between Coutts Alberta and Sweetgrass Montana. With long extensions on each end, the station allowed trans-border travellers an opportunity to enjoy a meal while clearing customs. It played this role from its completion by the Great Falls and Canada Railway in 1890 and served that function until 1917. In 2000 the building was moved to a property north of the village of Stirling, where it is now the Galt Historic Railway Park and the focus of a budding display of railway rolling stock.

The station museum recounts the stories of new arrivals, life at the station, and the history of station food service.

Emerson, Manitoba

While it is not a divisional station, the CP border station in Emerson, Manitoba, played a role above and beyond the country station. Its role here was to inspect goods entering Canada from neighbouring Minnesota, and it was built in 1914 to a singular plan. The wood building is topped by a wide, steep roof over a single storey with a bay window centrally placed. The roof extends right down to form an overhanging eave all around the structure. The exterior is wood shingle painted the traditional CPR red. Although closed and boarded, it is a protected station under the Heritage Railway Station Protection Act.

Empress, Alberta

The CPR station in Empress is a one of a kind. Displaying elements of a Chinese pagoda, it was built in 1914 to the CPR's plan X-12. The town was designated as a divisional point, despite the fairly small size of the station. The yards contained a roundhouse, water tower, and a coal dock.

The operator's bay window penetrates the bellcast roofline, where the tops of the window form an arch. As it was situated on the Alberta and Saskatchewan border, pressed metal wild roses, the symbol of Alberta, were incorporated into the ends of the roof ridge cap.

The divisional facilities were closed in the 1950s and the station vacated in 1972. The tracks are now gone as well. After being designated as a protected station in 1992 under the federal Heritage Railway Station Protection Act, the building has been repainted in the original yellow and red of the CPR to be used as a museum.

Hardisty, Alberta

The old wooden station in Hardisty, Alberta, was built in 1909 according to the CPR's prairie divisional style, known as branch line divisional station plan E-22-2. It was moved in 2008 to become a private business.

Kerrobert, Saskatchewan

Although the town is no longer a divisional point, a few of the yards remain as storage facilities for the CPR.

Now vacant, the branch-line divisional-station plan E-22-2 station is a designated heritage structure, as is the Canadian Bank of Commerce building a short distance away. The bank building, prefabricated in British Columba — as were many prairie banks — now serves as library. As part of the town planning that the CPR undertook in its railway towns, the remains of the boulevard still lead to the overgrown station grounds.

The station from Coutts, Alberta, served as a border customs station on the Montana border before being moved to Stirling as a museum.

Lanigan, Saskatchewan

Built in 1908 to the CPR's branch line divisional station plan E-22-2, the station in Lanigan is a long and low wooden structure dominated by a canopied street entrance topped with a bellcast roof. The main roof is similarly a bellcast shape that extends beyond the walls of the station to create a protective wraparound eave. The station was built at a time when Lanigan was the focus of five rail lines and was one of eight such structures built in this province. This particular plan, being intentionally more attractive, was kept for divisional points, even though they did not necessarily have a significant amount of additional space. It remains painted CPR red and has served as a museum and tourist information centre since 1995. A caboose rests beside the building.

La Riviere, Manitoba

Built in 1898 at La Riviere, Manitoba, in an effort to appeal to the Francophone population in parts of southern Manitoba, the CPR adopted a station style that featured a mansard roof. Inside, the waiting room was two storeys, while the freight shed was a single storey. Agents were quartered in a small upstairs apartment. Another interesting heritage element is the name hand-painted on the roof.

In 1908 the CPR added a roundhouse and a pump house, turning the village into a divisional point. While the roundhouse and pump house were demolished in the 1960s, the station was saved and moved to the Archibald Historical Museum a short distance away. Also in the museum village are three residences — two of which were once occupied by Nellie McClung — a historic church, and a large barn, which contains a number of display items. The station is also a designated provincial heritage site.

Minnedosa, Manitoba

This station was built in 1910 to serve a divisional point at this location following a fire to the original structure, and the CPR adopted a unique architectural style. Moving away from its pattern book, the brick building has wide eaves all around and three second-storey dormers, including a octagonal-shaped dormer above the operator's bay window. It was designated in 2001 as a municipal heritage site and today is owned by the town. A number of the yard sidings remain in use.

Moose Jaw, Saskatchewan

Moose Jaw, Saskatchewan, looms large in the railway lore of the Prairie provinces. The town grew from its selection as a divisional point on the CPR's historic main line to the west coast, a designation that the railway deliberately denied to nearby Regina. Early on, Moose Jaw's station had one of the CPR's more attractive station gardens, which attracted tourists. Visitors would occasionally comment on the pungent aroma of the garden's fertilizer that emanated from the waste from a nearby hotel.

While its first station was purely utilitarian and built for the sole purpose of getting the line running, the second station, erected in 1899, was one of the classic Châteauesque urban stations designed by the Maxwell brothers of Montreal, who were influenced by R.B. Pratt. The new structure was a long brick building, two-storeys and with a steep bellcast roofline. Higher peaks were featured at each end, and a third-storey peak dominated the central portion above the entrance, where small turrets marked the corners.

But as Moose Jaw was booming with more rail lines entering town, this grand building was soon out of date, and in 1928 yet another station appeared at the head of the main street. Designed by architect Hugh Jones of Montreal, the new and current building displays a decidedly Italianate style. In fact, its six-storey Campanile clock tower could well have been placed in an Italian village square. A steel canopy on decorative columns marks the entrance. Inside the high waiting room are wall medallions and reliefs of stone and terracotta. Arched windows, a clerestory, and pendant lighting all help illuminate the waiting hall. Passengers would enter through a steel entrance set off by limestone details like dentils and quoins. It has been designated as a provincial heritage site and listed as a protected station under the Heritage Railway Station Protection Act. Now closed as a station, it has become Station Square, inhabited by small businesses and a large liquor store.

Outlook, Saskatchewan

The station that now serves as the Outlook museum is one of only eight divisional stations that the CPR built to this rather pleasing design, known as standard plan X-13. It is distinguished by a porte-cochère over the street entrance, topped by a bellcast gable. A similar gable rests atop the operator's bay. It was built in 1909, shortly before the railway completed its massive High Level Bridge across the South Saskatchewan River, and it served as a major divisional point of the line's Moose Jaw to Edmonton branch. The divisional grounds contained the usual roundhouse, water tower, grain elevators, and stock yards. With the end of steam in the 1960s, all these buildings associated with the divisional yards were removed, and the station was reduced to local service, which ended in the 1970s. Still on its original site, the station was acquired by the museum in 1992, and it houses a variety of local artifacts.

Swift Current, Saskatchewan

The CPR established its next divisional point west of Moose Jaw at Swift Current. The buildings here were built between 1907 and 1912 to replace the original "Van Horne" station, and they represent one of the most complete railway heritage complexes on the Prairies.

The oldest of the three is the ticket office and passenger waiting rooms, and this was completed in 1907; it displays an eyebrow gable above the bay window, a feature on a number of CPR buildings. The next oldest is the two-storey dining room and telegraph office, which was finished in 1909 and enlarged in 1957; it includes a large gable on the trackside and smaller projecting gables in the hip roof. The most recent of the three is the express building, finished in 1912, and it displays few architectural embellishments.

While these buildings do not follow a pattern from other stations, they do exemplify CPR characteristics, with their low rooflines and brick exteriors. They still occupy their traditional trackside locations close to the downtown. The yards to the south of the buildings remain in full use, although no other divisional structures remain. The complex was designated under the HRSPA in 1991.

Westaskiwin, Alberta

At the Forks in Winnipeg, the Childrens' Museum now occupies the former NP&M repair shop.

Now a private business, the CPR station in Westaskiwin was built to a style that differed from the standard plan book. The first station here was built in 1891 on the Calgary and Edmonton Railway, and it reflected the standard plan used by that railway, namely a hip gable roof above the trackside section.

With the arrival of a junction with the CPR's Winnipeg to Edmonton main line, the first station was replaced with the larger, special-plan building that stands today. At the time of construction, the yards included a water tank, roundhouse, and grain elevators. Although the station is a straightforward two-storey structure, the roofline is distinguished by an "eyebrow" eve on the trackside portion. It is the only survivor from the many yard structures that once stood here. The Alberta Central Railway Museum uses a smaller version of this building a few kilometres to the southeast of the town as its gift shop and ticket office.

Wynyard, Saskatchewan

One of the CPR's oldest and most unusual prairie divisional stations remains in use in Wynyard, Saskatchewan.

Using a unique station pattern, the CPR's divisional station in Wynyard, Saskatchewan, displays a two-storey gambrel roof and gabled freight wing. As a divisional point, the grounds also included a round house. Built in 1909, the wooden structure was designated under the HRSPA in1992. By the end of 2011, portions were boarded up, and a set of new aluminum structures was added to accommodate the CPR employees.

THE WAY STATIONS
Andrew, Alberta

Along with a grain elevator, this CPR plan 14-A station has been moved from its original site to become a museum. A simple but attractive CPR design, it features a low, wide bellcast roof and a prominent gable above the operator's bay. It was one of the most common of the later station plans on the western prairies, with thirty-two built in Alberta and thirty-one in Saskatchewan. It was, however, a later plan, and most were built along the CPR's new branch lines between 1924 and 1930. The one in Andrew was built in 1928 and it closed in 1971.

The museum grounds in Andrew contain a typical CPR portable station and, naturally, a caboose. The town itself dates back to 1900, when Carey's store and the Andrew Hotel opened at the junction of the Winnipeg and Calgary-Pakan trails. When the station was built, all businesses relocated to the track side.

Arborg, Manitoba

Built in 1908, this standard CPR plan #5 station is one of the more common of the company's prairie stations, with its hip gable dormer on the second storey of the two-storey station. It was one of a string of stations on the ninety-kilometre Winnipeg to Arborg branch. It sits near its original site, where it now serves as the Evergreen

Regional Library. It was designated as a municipal heritage site in 1992 and retains its CPR red paint coating.

Bienfait, Saskatchewan

The CPR built this station in Bienfait, the heart of coal country in southeastern Saskatchewan, in 1908. The pattern was the line's near-universal design at the time, consisting of two storeys with a front hip gable encasing a pair of second-floor windows. As it was near the American border, prohibition days may have been the station's most active. Across the street stood the three-storey King Edward Hotel. That was where the Bienfait Export Liquor Company (also known as the "Boozorium"), a hotbed of bootlegging activity, operated. So profitable was the trade that the station attracted the attention of such Chicago gangsters as Dutch Schultz, who was sent by Capone himself with the purpose of meeting with one Paul Matoff, who had connections with the Bronfman liquor empire. On October 4, 1922, while he was inside the CPR station counting his money, Matoff was shot and killed. The hotel still stands, as does the now-relocated CPR station, which houses the Bienfait Coalfields Historical Museum. Displays depict the area's early coal mining days, which date back to 1895.

Brooks, Alberta

While the Brooks station itself now longer stands, the Brooks and District Museum contains the unusual little CPR station that stood at Duchess from 1920 until 1965. In 1984 it was acquired by the museum, which restored the structure and now displays it along with a CPR caboose and the log RCMP outpost building from Parvella. The wooden station style is simple, with few embellishments, and is not consistent with any of the railway's WLS plans. The operator's bay window is located at one corner of the structure, whereas it would normally be closer to the centre.

Castor, Alberta

Located in east central Alberta, Castor became a station stop on the CPR in 1909. Here, the railway built its standard plan 14-A station, which was namely a square, wooden, two-storey structure with a hip dormer enclosing a pair of windows to mark the agent's apartment. Following the closure of the station, the Castor Historical Society purchased the structure and relocated it to become a community museum. The exterior has been altered to obscure some of the architectural features.

Claresholm, Alberta

The attractive sandstone CPR stations now in Claresholm and High River began life in Calgary as part of that growing town's railway station needs. In fact, the two buildings, nearly identical, served together as the Calgary station. In 1910 the buildings were deemed inadequate for Calgary and both were dismantled, then one was moved to Claresholm and the other to High River, two towns close to each other to the south of Calgary. The CPR closed the Claresholm station in 1965. It has reopened as the Claresholm and District Museum and includes a caboose as part of its display. Both are designated provincial heritage sites.

Cut Knife, Saskatchewan

The CPR's grand old standard two-storey station now rests in Tomahawk Park at the west end of the village, along with a small number of other heritage structures. It was built in 1912 on the Wilkie to Lloydminister line just a year after the CPR introduced its WLS plan 4 — its most common on the prairies, with its simple peak-gabled dormer on the second-storey agent's apartment. The building was closed in 1973 and moved to the park.

Didsbury, Alberta

Now moved back from the busy tracks, the small station in this community north of Calgary is one of the few survivors of a CPR station plan known as plan X-6. The distinguishing characteristic of this style is the unusual mansard roof. It was constructed in 1902, about ten years after the CPR Calgary to Edmonton line was opened. Today, it is listed in the Alberta Register of Historic places. The station closed in 1977, and in 1991 the CPR deeded the building to the Lions Club, who agreed to move it back from the track and turn it around. It now serves as a Chamber of Commerce and scout/guide meeting hall. Four stations of this style were built in Alberta, two in Saskatchewan, and eleven in Manitoba.

Dunnotar, Manitoba

Soon after its line was completed, the CPR got into the recreation business, thanks to the enthusiasm of its builder and president William Cornelius Van Horne. He quickly realized the tourism potential of the Rocky Mountains, through which his line wound, and built hotels and resorts. In Manitoba the CPR inaugurated beach trains, one of which was ran from Selkirk to Winnipeg Beach at Dunnotar, where a small waiting room and open shelter were constructed in 1903. In 1906 the line continued farther, reaching Gimli in 1906 and then Riverton in 1914. Today, while the tracks are gone, the station that originally stood in Matlock a short distance away has been relocated to the Dunnotar station site and restored. A replica shelter was erected beside it.

Gunton, Manitoba

Built in 1944, the Gunton "waiting station" served as a shelter for CP passengers on its line in the Gunton area until the 1960s. It now serves as the Grosse Isle station stop for tourists enjoying the steam excursions of the Prairie Dog Central Railway.

Herbert, Saskatchewan

This community on the CPR's original main line has retained its 1910 two-storey wooden station, although it now has its back to the tracks. A feature of this two-storey wooden building is the afternoon "fasta," or Mennonite meal. A hip dormer covers a pair of second floor windows and indicates the location of the agent's quarters. The site also contains a model railway inside, and outside, a vintage snowplough, boxcar, and, surprise, a caboose.

High River, Alberta

The High River station is unique in a couple of respects. Along with the station at Claresholm, it is one of the rare examples of a stone station on the prairies. It was first built in Calgary. Designed in 1893 by the CPR architect Edward Colonna, it was one of a pair of similar structures that served as the Calgary station. But, by 1910, the station was inadequate for the booming town, and the stations were dismantled and relocated to High River and Claresholm, where they have today become regional museums.

The station in High River is the Museum of the Highwood. It has since recovered from a fire in 2010, which destroyed a portion of its collection. The stone structure exhibits a low roofline and two sets of doors on the street side, as well as a gable above the centre section. A CPR passenger coach sits beside the museum building.

Innisfail, Alberta

The focus of the extensive Innisfail Historic Village is the CPR's 1904 Bowden station. It was built in a plan more common to the line's eastern stations, with a steep bellcast roof and a hip gable dormer peeking through the roofline to indicate the agent's quarters. The station was built in Bowden in 1904 by the Calgary and Edmonton Railway (later the CPR) and moved to Innisfail in 1973. A replica of the Lacombe C&E station was constructed in that town on the opposite side of the tracks from where the original demolished station originally stood. It, too, displays the same steep roof and hip gable dormer as the Bowden station. It was built in 2007 and is a commercial centre known as Siding 12. Another replica C&E station was built in Penfold and it is also a commercial operation.

McCord, Saskatchewan

In 1926 the CPR began extending a branch line from Assiniboia to Coronach, laying out townsites where they erected a new standard plan station. Another example of the CPR's last line of rural station plans, the 1928 CPR station is now the McCord museum with a 1972 caboose to round out the ambience. The station was built to the CPR's WLS plan 14-A, with a wide bellcast roof and extended overhangs. The large half-timbered dormer dominates the roofline. The building retains its traditional CPR-red, wood-sided exterior. The station closed in 1970 and became the village museum, although, as per CPR's "heritage" policy, not on-site. In addition to the displays of local farm implements and quilts, the site offers a pair of original CPR privies. (Modern "lavs" are available as well.) A station with an identical style was moved from Coronach village to the local golf club.

Meath Park, Saskatchewan

Situated twenty-six kilometres northeast of Prince Albert, this station was built by the CPR during the 1930s, when they were extending their line between Prince Albert and Nipawin. The original settlement, which was primarily Polish and Ukrainian, had been established as early as 1906 but was about six kilometres to the south. The station here was known as a WLS-23, with a pagoda-style gable above the operator's bay. In the 1990s, the line was abandoned and the two grain elevators demolished. The station, a designated heritage property, is now the Ghost Rails Restaurant. The name comes from the abandoned CPR tracks and from the local stories that the building may be haunted. It stands on Railway Avenue, not far from its original site.

Morden, Manitoba

Now on the grounds of the Pembina Threshermen's Museum, the Morden CPR station was a rare CPR style found in only five other locations across the Prairies. Designed by R.B. Pratt in 1899, the steep roofline is topped with a flared peak and hipped eyebrow dormers, which earned this style the "Chinese Pagoda" moniker. Similar stations were found in Theodore, Saskatchewan; and Winkler, Boissevain, Hartney, Virden, and Kenton in Manitoba. The station was built in 1906, closed in the 1960s, and moved to the Threshermen's Museum in 1975. The office and waiting room retain many of their original features. Other buildings on the grounds include RCMP outpost log homes, a blacksmith, a church, and a general store.

Naicam, Saskatchewan

Another example of a station becoming a restaurant is the CPR station that turned into The Station Restaurant in 1974. Located on Highway 6 within Naicam, it has been renamed Venice House Pizza. The CPR built the station on its Watson to Melfort line in 1922 using one of its more attractive patterns, one in which the rooftop gable extends down to the first storey and across the full width of the facade. The CPR called it their Western Line A-3 pattern.

Nipawin, Saskatchean

Sitting on the western outskirts of the town of Nipawin, along the mandatory cabooses, is the sturdy station built according to the CPR's newly introduced western line A-3 station plan. This style was introduced in the 1920s and was first built in 1925 on the Tisdale to Prince Albert section. Closed in 1983, the station is now located in the Nipawin Forestry Museum and has been refurbished as the station would have originally looked.

Nokomis, Saskatchewan

Located now in the centre of the village, the Nokomis station, built in 1907 on the Strasburg to Lanigan section, is another of the CPR's standard two-storey wooden stations, which they built almost everywhere at that period. The station displays a hip dormer above a pair of windows indicating the agent's living quarters. Along with a caboose, the station is the focus of the Nokomis and District Museum, known as Junction City. Nokomis was in fact a junction between the CPR and the CNo.

Ogema, Saskatchean

The southern Saskatchewan town of Ogema once more has a station at the end of its main street. In conjunction with a concerted effort to celebrate its rail roots, Ogema has found and relocated from a nearby farm a station identical to that which the CPR had built in 1911 but removed in the 1960s. Originally from Simpson, the station has been fully restored to its original appearance and function. Part of that function will be the boarding point for the tour trains running on the Southern Prairie Railway, with a diesel from North Conway, New Hampshire, and a passenger coach from Gettysburg, Pennsylvania. The railway will strive to eventually operate a steam tour train. The restoration project also involves returning the town's railway water tower, which has been sitting on a nearby farm. The 114-kilometre short line, along which the tour train will operate as part of a short line operation, is owned by the communities that line it. The Deep South Pioneer Museum, whose transportation division spearheaded the station move, boasts of twenty-nine heritage structures moved in from nearby areas.

Okotoks, Alberta

The CPR built its station in Okotoks in 1928 in an atypical plan with two dormers on the second floor. The line from Calgary to Macleod was one of the CPR's first branch lines to follow the opening of its transcontinental route into Calgary. It replaced a smaller station that had originally been built in 1882 but was destroyed by fire. In 1981 the town purchased the structure and converted it into the community's art gallery. Much of the town itself has become a popular spot to visit, with its revitalized downtown area.

Paradise Valley, Alberta

Better known for its grain elevator interpretive centre, the community still retains its tiny station. To serve the many smaller villages around the prairies, the CPR pre-built a number of portable stations and transported them by flatcar to their destinations. Even though simple, this style, too, had a plan number, that being H-14-38A. The interior was three small rooms, including the waiting room, the ticket office, and the agent's small sleeping quarters. Being architecturally insignificant, few were saved, which makes the one in Paradise Valley relatively rare. It closed in the early 1990s and is now part of the elevator display complex.

Portage la Prairie, Manitoba

This prairie community in western Manitoba enjoys not just one but two heritage stations, and both are visible from each other. That of the CPR was designed by architect Edward Colonna in 1893, and it replaced a much simpler wooden structure that was derided for its dinginess. But, recognizing the growth potential of the prairie town, the CPR decided to erect a building consistent with its hopes for the town.

Its style is known as Richardsonian Romanesque, named after American architect H.H. Richardson, who designed many U.S. stations using stone and brick in a solid low-profile style. Many examples of his work still stand. The station in Portage la Prairie built of sandstone and yellow brick contains such typical features as rounded openings, arched windows and doors, and stone headstones and keystones. It remains one the most attractive of the surviving stations on the prairies, and one of

Edward Colonna, the CPR architect, designed the Portage la Prairie station in an elegant Richardsonian style, more common in the eastern U.S.

the oldest. It has been designated a federally protected station, and also as a municipal heritage site in 2004.

After the station was heavily damaged by a fire in 2002, a group of citizens formed a coalition to help restore the building. It is now the Canadian Pacific Heritage Railway Park and Interpretative Centre.

Riverton, Manitoba

In a project similar to that undertaken in Ogema, in 2000 the Riverton Heritage and Transportation Centre, north of Winnipeg, retrieved its CPR plan-4 WLS, originally built in 1917, from a nearby property and moved it back to its original location, where the community has restored it to its original condition to serve as a transportation and heritage centre. The building, once more repainted in CPR red, has a peak gable dormer encasing a pair of windows where the agent's quarters were located. Situated on Lake Winnipeg, the station had goods transferred to it from boats and winter tractor trains to serve Manitoba's more remote northern settlements. In fact, one of the boats is a restoration project as well.

Rocanville, Saskatchewan

The style that the CPR built in Rocanville was not a common one on the prairies, although many similar designs appeared in Ontario. Known as plan H-14-22, it was introduced into the CPR planbooks in 1903. A year later, the CPR laid out the town and built the station. The Rocanville station lies on its line between Virden, Manitoba, and Neudorf, Saskatchewan. A visit to Rocanville and the district museum will reveal the restored CPR station along with the Hillburn Church, the Schwantz Store, and the Prosperity School. The station is more typical of eastern stations, with its single storey, its long, low profile, and its wide, steep bellcast roof, punctured by a single hip gable

dormer. The collection is on the Canadian register of heritage places.

Rockglen, Saskatchewan

As the CPR's Assiniboia to Coronach branch line was being surveyed, a townsite named Valley City began to evolve where it was anticipated the CPR would locate its station. As was its practice, the CPR placed its station instead a short distance away, and the community followed it. The area was renamed Rockglen.

Built in 1928, the CPR station closed in 1962 and was an employee residence for the next eleven years. Purchased by the community in 1982, it now serves as the community's visitor centre. Nestled in a sweeping scenic valley, the area is gaining in popularity with artists and nature enthusiasts. As with other CPR stations along the new line, the station is a CPR plan 14-A, with a wide bellcast roof and a prominent dormer above the operator's bay window. Along with a small section of track and that inescapable caboose, the station still has its original wooden platform, an often overlooked aspect of a station's heritage features.

Rosthern, Saskatchewan

Perhaps fewer than a dozen railway stations on the prairies were constructed with the rare mansard style roof. La Riviere in Manitoba and Didsbury in Alberta are two others that survive. The station in Rosthern, Saskatchewan, was built by the CPR in 1902 during its brief ownership of the Qu'Appelle, Long Lake and Saskatchewan Railway, from 1896 until the CNo acquired the line in 1906. The CNR continued to use the building until 1981, when the railway sold it to the municipality. The station remains near its original site and now serves as the village art gallery, known as the Station Arts Centre, but it also features a theatre and a tea room. Its distinctive features have been carefully restored and preserved. The tracks remain in use to serve a pair of remaining grain elevators and are operated by the Carlton Trail Railway.

Shandro, Alberta

This village that contains the Shandro Pioneer Village and Museum also has the CPR station from Willingdon, Alberta. The single-storey station with the gable over the bay window was built in 1928 along the CPR's line from Lloydminster to Calgary; this was to the CPR's common plan 14-A. The grounds also feature a wooden Ukrainian Orthodox church and a small collection of early pioneer structures.

Strasbourg, Saskatchewan

The station, which the CPR built in 1906 on the Lanigan line north of Regina, was one of dozens built to its standard rural plan typified by the two full storeys with a hip gable dormer that encases two windows and delineates the agent's quarters. The building has an unusually long freight shed, which reflects the high amount of freight traffic that emanated from this location. Following the station's closing in 1970, the town acquired the building for its museum and moved it a short distance back from the track.

Strathclair, Manitoba

The station in Strathclair, Manitoba, is a rare surviving example of a station built in 1900 by the Manitoba and Northwestern Railway, which was later absorbed by the CPR. The main orientation of the station is perpendicular to the tracks. The station it is a full two storeys and contains a hipped gable roof. The plan was also used by the CPR for many of its early structures along the Calgary to Edmonton and Fort Macleod lines and the Qu'Appelle, Long Lake and Saskatchewan line. A lengthy extension for freight lies to the side. Now owned by the municipality, this wooden structure was designated by the province as a municipal heritage property in 2003.

Theodore, Saskatchewan

This unusual station is one of only five designed by the CPR's architect R.B. Pratt in this style in Saskatchewan and is the only one to survive in that province, although another fine example lies in Virden, Manitoba. Although this style of station is typically two-storeys, the peak forms a pagoda-style profile. A number of prairie stations adopted a modified Chinese element to their roofline, and Theodore was one of the larger such structures. It was relocated in the 1970s to the centre of the village, first as a seniors centre and later a museum. It is now a designated municipal heritage property. Other examples survive at Virden (on site) and Morden (relocated).

Unity, Saskatchewan

Built in 1909 and situated three kilometres north of Unity, the CPR station was constructed in the common style of the period, with a small peak gable set into the second storey roof, encasing a two-window dormer. The wooden building, still sporting its CPR red paint, is now the focus of an extensive heritage park, which includes a variety of heritage buildings such as churches, stores, and schools. A steam engine is on display inside a Quonset hut.

Vegreville, Alberta

After serving for many years as a bottle depot, the Vegreville CPR station, built in 1928 on a line between Camrose and Willingdon, has now become a restaurant. Unlike many of the CPR stations across the prairies, this small station was built with brown brick on a concrete block base. It has a small gable above the operators bay and two dormers on the rear roof. The tracks have been abandoned since 1976.

Virden, Manitoba

The CPR station in this western Manitoba town is one of the most stunning on the Prairie landscape. Designed in 1899 by CPR architect R.B. Pratt, the two-storey structure offers a most unusual peak to its steep roof, reminiscent of a Chinese pagoda. Indeed, this and similar stations in Theodore, Saskatchewan, and Morden, Manitoba, have earned the nickname "Chinese Pagoda." Similar eaves extend over the two second storey dormers, and beak-like extensions decorate the two hip gable ends of the station. Of all the stations built to this pattern, the one in Virden is the only one built using stone, and is the only surviving example to remain on-site. It has been designated both federally and provincially as heritage structure.

OTHER RAIL LINES

Northern Alberta Railway

Well to the northwest of Edmonton, another region of the prairies began to experience a surge of settlement: the Peace Region. In 1909 the Peace River country was opened to settlement in the hope that the Canadian Northern and the Grand Trunk Pacific Railways would follow through on their promise to extend their lines into the region. In 1916 the Central Canada Railway Corporation built a line to the Peace Region, linking with the Edmonton, Dunvegan and British Columbia Railway at McLennan. Following sale to the CNR and CPR railways, the line was renamed the Northern Alberta Railway in 1930.

Dawson Creek

Dawson Creek's Northern Alberta Railway (NAR) Park contains the 1931 NAR station museum constructed in the CPR's final prairie design and houses the South Peace Historical Society Museum. The park also celebrates Mile 0 of the Alaska Highway and contains an art gallery in the relocated 1948 AWP grain elevator.

Fahler, Alberta

When the NAR reached Fahler, Alberta, deep in the Peace country in 1915, the community's first station appeared. It was replaced by a second and then, in 1930, by a CPR station plan known as 14-A, with its wide, low bellcast roofline and prominent gable. It was sold in 1972, and now, repainted in blue, it is a tourist information centre near the Fahler campground.

Peace River, Alberta

In 1916 the wooden storey-and-a-half station at Peace River was built by the Edmonton, Dunvegan and British Columbia Railway (ED&BC), which in 1929 became part of the Northern Alberta Railway (NAR), operated jointly by CNR and CPR. In 1980 CN became the sole operator and closed the station the following year. Passenger service, however, ended well before that, in 1956. The station originally offered two waiting rooms: the general waiting room and the Ladies' Waiting Room. The latter was enlarged and converted to a general waiting room, while what had been the general waiting room became the freight room. Following a fire in 1986, the Northern Alberta Railways Association acquired the damaged structure and, over the following five years, restored it a 1920s appearance. While CN trains still use the line, the station is now a tourist information centre with much of the interior flooring and wainscoting restored. It remains on its original site and is also a provincial heritage site.

Sexsmith, Alberta

The ED&BC Railway reached Sexsmith in 1916, and the community quickly became the focus for grain equipments, boasting a row of nine elevators. In 1928 the railway replaced the original station with a more elegant structure. Constructed of wood and painted a distinctive maroon colour, the storey-and-a-half building was distinguished by its bellcast roof with gable ends and dormers to house the agent and his family. In the 1970s, the station closed and was moved away to house a farm implement dealership. In the 1980s, the Sexsmith Museum Society acquired and returned the building to its original site, where they restored its original features. In 1994 it was declared a municipal heritage resource, and it now serves as a museum.

Several other NAR stations do survive, but most are now in different locations, where they have become farm buildings or houses.

St. Boniface Greater Winnipeg Water District Station

One of the more delightful heritage stations on the prairies is the attractive stone railway station, which continues to serve the Greater Winnipeg Water District (GWWD) Railway. Designed by local architect William Fingland, the new station was built in 1929 to replace the earlier 1919 wooden structure. The interior was laid out to contain a waiting room, baggage room, cold storage area, and the station master's equipment. The roofline features a cross-gable through the middle to form a projecting bay with parapet gables on either side. The red, grey, and pink granite, quarried from along the line, is laid out in

a cyclopean pattern, with stone detailing on the corner gables and windows. Semi-circular windows are set into the end gables and the bay gable as well. Raised letters on the northwest gable read, GWWD RAILWAY STATION.

On display in front of the St. Boniface GWWD station is *Railbus #205*, which once carried passengers and workers along the line. It was one of only six manufactured in 1921 by the J.G. Brill company and was used mainly for maintenance of way. It replaced a "Mack" car built in 1928 but destroyed by fire in 1991. Passenger service has been discontinued since 1982. The building is located on Plinquet Street in an industrial area of St. Boniface. The GWWD built a string of flag stations along its line, most of which have since been demolished or relocated.

Nearby, the simple single-storey former-CN station now serves as the Resto Gare Restaurant, and it features a passenger coach for extra seating.

The Mountain Stations

Although the Rocky Mountains do not form part of the Prairies, the Alberta stations located at the gateways to this scenic range are among Canada's most elegant and illustrate the intention of the rail companies to earn income from not just grain shipments but tourism as well.

Jasper CNR

This fine station was built by the CNR in 1926 as part of the government's efforts to attract visitors to Jasper National Park, and to the CNR's own lodge. Designed by the rail company's architects in Winnipeg who used an "Arts and Crafts" style, its roof is a series of varied, steep dormers, while the base and pillars use attractive cobblestones. Inside, visitors find stone fireplaces, heavy beamed ceilings, elegant lighting, and built-in furnishings. Not too surprisingly, it is now a federally protected station, and one of the most attractive on VIA Rail's line. Not only does VIA Rail's *Canadian* pause here for an hour and a half, but it is also the departure point for the *Skeena*, part of VIA's equally scenic service through the mountains to Prince George and Prince Rupert.

Banff CPR

This elegant structure was built by the CPR in 1910 to complement the efforts to attract travellers to the Banff Springs Hotel, one of the grandest in the CPR's chain of hotels. A number of large dormers line the roof, while a stone-and-wood finish mark its exterior, along with wood shingling and half timbering — all meant to reflect the natural experience that the CPR was promoting. Although no longer a stop for VIA Rail, it does give travellers on the *Rocky Mountaineer* or the CPR's *Royal Canadian Pacific* a taste of this "Arts and Crafts" style of grand station. It was designated as a federally protected station in 1991. The original station had been constructed east of today's site, but was moved in 1888 with the opening of the hotel. Those not travelling by train may enjoy the station's rail-themed restaurant, the Caboose.

Lake Louise CPR

Another of the CPR's tourist destinations, the Lake Louise station was built in 1910 in conjunction of the Chateau Lake Louise a short distance away. Its distinguishing characteristics are its peeled log construction and large windows built to allow views of the mountain scenery. No longer a stop for trains, it now functions as a popular restaurant. Next to the building sit a grouping of vintage CPR coaches. The first station, also built of log, was named Laggan and now resides in Calgary's Heritage Park.

Chapter Four

The Castles of the Lines: The Railway Hotels

Canada's early rail travellers needed places to stay overnight and sometimes longer periods. These were often itinerant salesmen. Descending from the hissing coaches, likely tired and hungry, they didn't want to endure a long walk, luggage in hand, to their night's accommodation, especially if they were carting wares to display. For this reason, hotels were invariably a vital adjunct to the railway station landscape. And the railways made sure there was space for one nearby.

But the railways, caught up in their own sense of grandeur, and also wanting to earn extra income from luring travellers to their better destinations, often built the hotels themselves — and the grander the better. Put the blame on William Cornelius Van Horne, the crusty president of the CPR. Realizing the stunning beauty of the Rocky Mountains, which rose suddenly from the stark prairies, and spurred by the surprising discovery of hot springs in those mountains, he built the Banff Springs Hotel. It was just one of several his company would create, usually in the stunning Château style, with steeply pitched rooflines and towers and turrets. Other rail lines followed suit, and these buildings stand as being among the grandest elements of the prairie railway landscapes.

The Hotel MacDonald, Edmonton

Built in 1915 by the Grand Trunk Pacific Railway, the "Mac" was designed by the architectural firm of Ross and MacFarland as a Château-style hotel, typified by its steeply pitched copper roof. Situated on a high bluff overlooking the North Saskatchewan River, its terrace and garden were a popular feature. Its location at the opposite end of 100th Street from the station ensured the railway a dominant visual presence of Edmonton's early commercial core. The firm also designed similar grand hotels for the GTR and GTP, including the Fort Garry in Winnipeg and the Château Laurier in Ottawa.

A later sixteen-storey addition so detracted from the ambience of the original seven-storey building that it was removed in 1983. Then, in 1988, the Canadian Pacific hotels bought and restored the old building, and today "the Mac" has regained much of its original elegance.

Ornamental plaster work decorates the high ceilings of both the lobby and Confederation Lounge, while eight historic provincial crests adorn the mezzanine. Meanwhile, the Wedgewood Room has retained its original plaster frescos.

Perhaps the most rewarding result of the restoration was when the false ceiling was removed from the Empire Ballroom to reveal an eight-metre high ceiling with a classical "Chase" scene painted on it. In earlier times, unescorted ladies and gents used separate rooms; the Ladies Drawing Room for the ladies and the Gentlemen's Writing Room, now the Jasper Room, for the men. The latter was decorated with rich oak panelling and stained-glass windows.

Behind the building, a formal garden sits high above the wide valley of the North Saskatchewan River. The building, now part of the Delta chain, still retains a magnificent garden overlooking the North Saskatchewan River. It was designated in 1984 as a municipal heritage resource.[8]

The GTP's Failed Chateau Qu'Appelle, Regina

For Regina, the GTP proposed a grand hotel at the corner of 16th (now College Avenue) and Albert Streets in downtown Regina. In 1910 the GTP had erected a station and roundhouse near a residential area and wanted to add a grand railway hotel in nearby parkland. Because the station had been built in a residential area, the city council came under fire for considering a hotel in one the city's more popular parks, Wascana Park. But the GTP got the go-ahead anyway.

The garden of the Hotel MacDonald in Edmonton overlooks the North Saskatchewan River.

The plans would incorporate the style into the name by calling it the Chateau Qu'Appelle, named after the Qu'Appelle Valley. In 1913 construction began and soon the steel skeleton stood seven storeys in the air. But the war intervened and construction halted. By the time the war ended and peace was declared, the GTP (and the CNo as well) were out of money. Both rail lines were absorbed into the newly created Canadian National Railway, which showed an interest in completing the building, but the federal government did not share that interest, and the hotel remained unfinished. Had the Chateau Qu'Appelle been successful, then Saskatchewan's "Queen City" would have had its grand hotel in true Scottish baronial style.

Later, in 1927, when the CPR decided to locate a grand hotel in the provincial capital, they acquired the unused girders from the Chateau Qu'Appelle and used them to construct the Hotel Saskatchewan.

The CPR's Hotel Saskatchewan, Regina

Located in downtown Regina, this railway hotel moved away from the grand Château style so favoured by the CPR and GTP in their earlier years, and it exudes a simpler, more classic flavour.

Following the failure of the Chateau Qu'Appelle, the city council lobbied the CPR to come up with a "grand hotel" for their city. Using some of the girders from the Qu'Appelle, and tyndall stone for the facade, the hotel was ready to open in 1927. It represented a more contemporary style of building.

Inside, however, the building is as elegant as any of its Châteauesque cousins, with an elaborate lobby and a Royal Suite, home to any visiting royalty. The Brighton Boardroom and the Regency Ballroom, as well as the Monarch's Lounge, all reflect the royal aspirations of this grand hotel. The Royal Suite is specifically designed with royal elegance in mind. The hotel today is part of the Radisson chain.

Winnipeg's Fort Garry Hotel

As happened all across the prairies during railway's heyday, the hotel and usually the station became the grandest structures in the city. While the CPR had built its own hotel, the Royal Alexander, adjacent to its Winnpeg station, and the Northern Pacific and Manitoba (NP&M, later the Canadian Northern) constructed a Château-style hotel atop its first station, the Grand Trunk Pacific undertook to construct the Fort Garry Hotel.

Designed by famous railway architectural firm of Ross and MacFarland, the thirteen-storey landmark opened in 1913. Using Indiana limestone, the design displays its Château elements primarily along the roofline, where the slope is steeply pitched, with multiple peaks and dormers. At the entrance, the stone stairs, brass railings, and copper canopy lead to a two-storey foyer, where the arches and pillars that surround the mezzanine display the national and provincial emblems. The floor is marble inlay and the stairs are marble as well, with iron and bronze balustrades. Piers and mouldings are trimmed in gold, while a bronze railing surrounds the mezzanine. The action, however, takes place on the seventh floor, where the oak-lined two-storey ceiling contains decorative lanterns. Arched openings with French doors lead to such grand rooms as the Concert Ballroom and the Crystal Ballroom, where the vaulted ceiling offers crystal chandeliers as well as oak columns and stained-glass transoms. And it sits within a block of the city's grand Union Station.

The CPR's Royal Alexandra Hotel and a long-forgotten hotel, the Hotel Manitoba, are but two of the lost railway hotels. The Hotel Manitoba was built by a rail line that has also been forgotten: the NP&M, which operated between the Forks and Emerson. The company built a seven-storey Château-style hotel, which included its station and offices as well, at the corner of Water and Main Streets. Completed in 1890 with luxurious accommodations and Château-style towers, it lasted only nine years, burning in 1899. Soon afterward, the CNo assumed control of the NP&M railway.

The Royal Alexandra Hotel was designed by the CPR's chief architects Edward and William Maxwell and was opened in 1906. Considered an upscale facility, it operated until 1967 and was demolished four years later. The interior of its dining room can still be seen if one travels to the Canadian Museum of Rail Travel in Cranbrook, British Columbia. The fine oak carvings, including the oak fireplace, were among more than a hundred separate sections from the hotel's grand café obtained by the museum after two decades of storage. They were reassembled by the museum in 2004, now in a new shell as the "Royal Alexandra Hall."

Sadly, the same cannot be said for the massive murals that the CPR commissioned prominent artist Frederick Challener to prepare for the hotel dining room. These evocative paintings, which measured 3.5 by 3.5 metres, decorated the hotel's vast dining room and depicted the life of both the aboriginal populations and the early settlers. Although the CPR donated the artwork to the province, removing and restoring them proved complicated and expensive. Ultimately, four were restored and briefly displayed at the Winnipeg Art Gallery in 1973. Sadly, only one remains on public view, in the Manitoba Archives, and the others were put in storage.

The whereabouts of the unrestored murals is unknown. The seven-storey building stood at the corner of Higgins and Main, close to the surviving former CPR station.[9]

The CPR's Palliser Hotel, Calgary

Unlike most of the CPR's other grand railway hotels, the Palliser, although no less spectacular, was designed by architect Lawrence Gotch in what architects called the Edwardian Commercial style. When guests attended the grand opening in June 1914, they were treated to views of marble columns and floors, oak panelling, and hand-woven rugs. The Renaissance Revival Rotunda consists of Tennessee marble flooring and Italian marble columns.

A special celebration of the hotel's distinctive railway heritage is the more recent Canadian Pacific Pavilion, reminiscent of CP station designs. Here, a twelve-metre-high ceiling with marble floors is connected to the Great Hall, a 150-metre extension that houses the classic coaches of the *Royal Canadian Pacific* train. When the luxury coaches are in town, diners can book one of the vintage CPR business cars for meals.

The Rimrock Restaurant contains an eleven-metre mural by artist Charles Bell. The restaurant's historic fireplace was saved from removal to facilitate kitchen access, and it remains one of the hotel's more historic features. Access to the Calgary CPR station was through the hotel until passenger service to Calgary was eliminated by the government of Brian Mulroney. Travellers on the CPR's vintage *Royal Canadian Pacific* tour train can still board here, however.

The Bessborough Hotel, Saskatoon

This elegant Château-style classic stands high above the South Saskatchewan River, where, with its steep roof and frequent dormers, it has earned the nickname "the castle on the river." The grand building is a surprising latecomer to the Château-hotel era in Canada, having opened only in 1935.

The railways, however, had arrived long before, with the CPR showing up in 1889 and the Canadian Northern in 1905. The CNo station, modelled after the one in Dauphin, with a high pyramid roof flanked by two wings, stood at the head of 21st Street. But the town lacked a comparable grand hotel. In 1927, when the CPR opened its Hotel Saskatchewan in Regina, local business interests lobbied the Canadian National Railway to provide a

Known as the "castle on the river," the CNR's Château-style Bessborough Hotel in Saskatoon was not completed until the 1930s.

comparable structure. As a result, architect J.S. Archibald went to work outdoing his CPR rivals with his soaring castle-like design. Following Archibald's death, John Schofield, the CN architect who designed several other stations during the thirties, took over.

Finally, in 1935, Saskatoon got a look at its new château. It was named after Canada's then governor general, Sir Vere Ponsonby, 9th Earl of Bessborough. Interestingly, the vice regal suite sits not at the top, nor facing the river, but rather on the 3rd floor, facing down the main street toward the CN station. Subsequent "improvements," as often happens, covered many of the hotels more decorative features. Restoration began in 1999 and lasted five years, unveiling original ceiling moulds and plaster reliefs, and the original terrazzo floor was restored.

Stretching from the street side of the hotel, 21st Street has been landscaped and its many heritage buildings preserved. And at the end of the street, there stands a replica of the CNo's 1905 station, which had been demolished in 1952. The replica houses a new downtown mall. But more than that, its facade, dominating one end of the main street, and the hotel the other, helps to celebrate a heritage railway landscape found in few other communities.

The Strathcona, Edmonton

Not all the hotels built by railways on the prairies were grand châteaus. Some were simple, but no less historic. Such is the case with the Strathcona Hotel in Edmonton's Old Strathcona heritage district.

In 1891 the CPR's Calgary and Edmonton Railway reached the south bank of the North Saskatchewan River and went no farther, much to the dismay of Edmontonians. Here, it located its station, and, to accommodate its passengers, built a hotel across the street. The three-storey wooden structure, initially called the Edmonton House, was until 1904 the area's largest hotel, accommodating newly arrived immigrants as well as hosting many community functions. It was enlarged in 1904 and again in 1907. Then, in 1913, when the CPR built the High Level Bridge over the river and added a new station in downtown Edmonton, the importance of the Strathcona dwindled. When prohibition was imposed in 1918, it became the Westminster's Ladies College. But when prohibition ended just six years later, thirsty Strathconians began pounding at the doors, and it once more became a tavern and hotel — a role it plays today.

Here, in conjunction with the CPR's grand Strathcona station and a heritage main street, the hotel helps to create one of the stronger railway heritage townscapes in the region. One of the last of the wooden hotels, it was designated a provincial heritage resource in 2001.

Moose Jaw's River Street Hotel Row: A Heritage Lost

In August 2000, Moose Jaw's city council announced a $470,000 upgrade to the city's historic "hotel row," River Street. Two blocks from the CPR station, the street grew into a strip of hotels, many of which harboured ladies of the evening and catered to the lustier instincts of single railway men and visiting salesmen. The new initiative would involve installing decorative sidewalks, street lamps, and an iron-arched gateway above each sidewalk. In addition, the historic buildings would receive a much-needed facelift.

In his public statement, the city mayor, Ray Boughen, boasted that the project would be "a great addition to our city as a tourist destination." Among those historic properties was the Brunswick Hotel, a designated heritage property. By 2003 the sidewalks lamps and gateway were all in place. The revitalization, the mayor noted, would play a role in the 2005 centennial celebration of the province.

The historic row of three- and four-storey hostelries grew up with the development of the site as a major CPR divisional point and repair terminal. Train crews, travelling salesmen, and job-seekers crammed into few spaces available. When the boom times quieted down, and the rowdies of an earlier era had either married or moved on, River Street became a seedy row of dingy taverns and flop houses. Nonetheless, their role in the early history of Moose Jaw's growth gave them a distinctive heritage prominence.

Unfortunately, within a few years of the announcement, a developer had made clear his plans to demolish not just the Brunswick but the entire historic street. Outraged citizens created a Facebook page to oppose the demolition.

In 2009 the city stripped the Brunswick Hotel of its heritage status and allowed the developer to proceed with the demolition. As the new mayor, Dale McBean, lamented, that while to see the hotel removed would be "sad," it had seen "the ravages of time."

Chapter Five

The Fall of the Prairie Sentinels: The End of the Grain Elevators

Fleming, Saskatchewan: The Last One Standing

There is an episode in the popular sitcom *Corner Gas* when Hank Yarbo, the town "doofus" (played by Frank Ewanuick), decides to burn down an old shed so that his Lego replica of the fictional town of Dog River would be accurate. As he dances gleefully around the smouldering structure, he does not know that it had been the town's original and most historic structure. To him, it was just an "old shed."

It seems that Canada's prairie provinces may have their share of "Hank Yarbos." At 4:00 a.m. on the morning of Tuesday, February 7, 2010, a truck driver noticed a fiery glow lighting up the dark Saskatchewan sky. He immediately alerted the volunteer fire department in the town of Fleming, but it was too late to save Canada's oldest grain elevator. Built in 1895 by the Lake of the Woods Milling Company, it was a rare square grain elevator topped by a cupola and could hold thirty-two thousand bushels of wheat. It had been slated for demolition in 2000, but the town of just ninety-five residents managed to raise $140,000 to save it and have it declared a national historic site. After years of volunteer work, the building was converted to an elevator interpretive centre and would have opened in only a few months. In April 2011 two "Hank Yarbos," men aged twenty and twenty-two, were arrested and charged with arson.

Years before this fiery fiasco, many heritage lovers across the prairies were concerned over the rate at which these country icons, often called the "Prairie Sentinels," were disappearing. In fact, so concerned was the Saskatchewan Heritage Foundation that it undertook an inventory of the province's surviving elevators, with special emphasis on the most historic of all: the wooden elevators. It discovered that, over a ten-year period alone, 1999–2009, the number of wooden grain elevators had fallen from eight hundred to a mere 420. The report was published in February 2010.[10] More than eighty-five of those still standing date from before 1930, while fourteen or so date from before the First World War. With fire having destroyed the 1895 elevator in Fleming, the oldest elevator in Saskatchewan became that in Sintaluta, having been built in 1904, while the elevator in Creelman was added just two years later.

Grain shipping began in 1876, when wheat was sent from Manitoba by barge along the Red River to Saint Paul, Minnesota, the then-head of rail for travel to and from the territory.

The first prairie grain elevator was built in 1879 in Niverville, Manitoba, and was round in shape. Prior to that, grain was simply stored in flat sheds and shovelled from wagons. But the round shape proved impractical, and these sheds were replaced by square or rectangular elevators, the form that has become such a landscape icon. The first was built in 1881 in Gretna, Manitoba.

Elevators were solidly built using two-by-six planks atop one another so that the walls could withstand the pressure of the grain. Each elevator would contain sixteen to eighteen bins. As the grain arrived, it would be weighed, graded, then poured into buckets, which would elevate the grain and then pour it into the proper bin. At first this was accomplished by horse power, but that was soon replaced with the gasoline engine.

As the three major rail companies extended their branch lines through the prairies, more than three hundred elevator companies were formed, and by 1920 more than two thousand elevators had been built, with capacities ranging from thirty thousand bushels to forty-five thousand. After the Grand Trunk Pacific and the Canadian Northern Railways went bankrupt and folded into the Canadian National Railways, elevator building continued, their numbers peaking in the late 1930s at more than 5,700.

From the time that the Canadian government granted the CPR a monopoly over grain shipping, prairie farmers resented the railway and the large grain companies. To the farmers, it quickly became clear that the railway was frequently refusing to load a farmer's grain directly onto its cars, forcing the farmers to go through the monopolistic grain companies. A court case in Manitoba in 1902 finally granted the farmers the right to load their grain directly onto the rail cars, which the railways declined to supply in sufficient quantities. This prompted the grain growers to go even further, and in 1925 they began to form their own cooperatives, which were known as "pools." By the time of the depression, provincial wheat pools controlled most of the elevators.

As settlement moved west and into Alberta, the first elevator was erected along the Calgary and Edmonton Railway at Strathcona in 1895. By 1906 Alberta could still count only forty-three elevators, although just six years later there were 280. In 1923 the Alberta Wheat Pool (AWP) entered the picture to provide competition for the hated private elevator companies and at its height held 879 elevators, while the province as a whole contained more than 1,780 such structures. But consolidation and branch line abandonment, along with too-frequent local disinterest in heritage preservation, reduced that number to a mere 176 in 2010.

Time has not been kind to the historic symbol of the prairie provinces. Their distinctive shape and structure has made most of them impractical for any form of adaptive re-use other than as grain elevator museums, and during the closing years of the 20th century, more than 80 percent of those "prairie sentinels" came down. Almost too late, westerners came to realize the value of what they were losing, and many communities have begun to save them, often opening them as interpretive centres, some with their own tea room.

ALBERTA

The Province of Alberta has designated a dozen grain elevators as provincial heritage resources, making them eligible for provincial assistance. These are located in Andrew, Radway, Leduc, Meeting Creek, Paradise Valley, Castor, and Scandia, as well as three in Rowley and a pair in St. Albert. Many local municipalities have also declared them as municipal heritage properties, and local groups have simply proceeded with preservation on their own.

The Prairie Elevator Museum, Acadia Valley,

In 1989 the active little historical society in the town of Acadia Valley, Alberta, bought the old Alberta Wheat Pool grain elevator — the last of the three that once stood in the village — for a dollar and set to work to convert it into a grain elevator interpretive centre, one of several appearing across the prairies. Using student guides and videos, visitors learns how grain is sorted, graded, weighed, and then loaded into the hopper cars for their trip to elevators complexes at the Lakehead. There is also information on how to identify various types of grain. A tea room operates during the summer months.

Andrew Grain Elevator

This iconic landmark was built by the Alberta Wheat Pool in 1928 and had a capacity of forty thousand bushels before it became inadequate in 1985. At that time, a pair of annexes were added to each end, more than tripling its capacity. Since that time, it has been further enhanced with the addition of a new drive shed, power train, and modern dust collection system. It has also been added to the Alberta registry of historic places. Although the elevator remains in full operation, the Andrew and District Historical Archives Museum Society will guide visitors through the site. The CPR station has also been preserved in this community.

The Castor Grain Elevator

When Alberta premier Alexander Rutherford convinced the CPR to extend its tracks eastward from Stettler in 1909, a new town named Castor sprang up at the line's temporary terminus, and here in 1910, the Alberta Pacific Grain Company erected a thirty-five thousand bushel grain elevator. In 1913 the line was extended into Saskatchewan, where it would link with the cross-country

grain route to the massive elevators at Fort William. As a result, in 1917 a larger forty-five thousand bushel elevator began operation. Ultimately, Castor would add four more elevators, making for an elevator row of five. While this structure, now listed on the Alberta registry of historic places, is the last of the row to survive, it still contains the drive shed, Gerber wheel, and conveyor.

In the 1990s, the United Grain Growers closed the elevator. At that time, two other elevators still stood, but they were subsequently demolished. The Canada's Historic Places inventory lists it as being the oldest of its type in Alberta. The Castor and District Museum, which acquired the elevator, has also moved historic rail cars onto the track next to it. These include a double-deck livestock car, a grain boxcar, and a grain tank car. The elevator was declared a provincial heritage resource in 2004.

Dawson Creek's Elevator Art Gallery

In 1931 the Northern Alberta Railway (NAR) arrived in the fertile regions northwest of Edmonton. Soon, the tracks of Dawson Creek were in the shadow of eight grain elevators. By 1950 those elevators were exporting more grain than any other community on the prairies. But, even as early as the 1980s, centralization was eliminating the grain elevators, and Dawson Creek soon had only two remaining.

In 1982 a group was formed to save at least one of the two surviving sentinels and use it for an art gallery. While the Alberta Wheat Pool agreed to sell the structure for $2, it also required the town to move it. Since the 1948 elevator stood more than thirty metres high, it was no easy feat, nor did it enjoy universal approval within the community. Funds were found from government grants, community fundraising, the Devonian Foundation; in 1983, on its new cement foundation, the Elevator Art

Gallery opened. It is situated in NAR Park, home also to the 1931 NAR station.

Kinuso

When the Dunvegan Railway made its way from Edmonton to the Peace Country, it established a townsite it called Swan River. Years later it became the village of Kinuso. The old grain elevator in Kinuso is not just an early structure, but the only one left that still shows the United Grain Growers (UGG) lettering. In 1974, when the UGG closed it, they sold it to a local business for grain storage. The owners continued to maintain it, eventually donating it to the Kinosayo Museum. With a lease from CN and a provincial heritage grant in hand, the museum began the job of re-shingling the looming structure.

Leduc Elevator

Although listed on the Alberta Registry of Historic Places, the Leduc elevator is a newcomer, having been built only in 1978. What renders it historically significant is the fact that it is one of the last single-wood crib grain elevators ever built in the province. Concrete and steel have dominated the prairie skyline in their place. Despite its historic appearance, the Leduc elevator is modern in every other respect, including power train ventilation and distribution systems.

Mayerthorpe Elevator

Although recent by historical standards, the 1966 Alberta Wheat Pool elevator in Mayerthorpe is nonetheless listed on the Alberta Register of Historic Places. Its heritage value lies in its being one of the later wood composite elevators and is the last of a half-dozen elevators built in this community. It is connected to an annex that had been constructed in 1940. In 1928 the AWP erected its first elevator here, on what was to have been the CNo's line to Grande Prairie, but it took the arrival of the CNR in the 1920s to finally bring tracks into Mayerthorpe. Work was underway as of 2011 to develop an interpretive centre in the elevator.

The Meeting Creek Elevators

Located in a shallow, scenic valley, the railway village of Meeting Creek presents one of Alberta's more photogenic railway landscapes. With its preserved Canadian Northern Railway station, the village can claim two preserved Alberta Pacific Grain Company elevators. While not the province's oldest, they were added between 1914 and 1917. When the Central Western Railway abandoned the track in 1997, they donated that which lay in front of the station and the grain elevators to the Canadian Northern Society, which administers the site. Much of the original equipment remains in place in the elevators, which are now listed on the Alberta Registry of Historic Places.

Nanton Elevators: The Canadian Grain Elevator Discovery Centre

Although technically not a "row" (which consists of four or more wooden elevators) Nanton's three surviving elevators, built between 1927 and 1929, were acquired by a concerned citizens group, the Save One Society, to create the Canadian Grain Elevator Discovery Centre. But the group went even further and in 2006 began work on the Nanton Heritage Railway, with railway rolling stock resting on two hundred metres of track. After considerable work by dedicated volunteers, one of the three elevators opened for tours, and the public can see how one of the Prairies' most beloved symbols functioned in practice.

Paradise Valley's "Climb Through Time"

The Alberta Wheat Pool elevator in Paradise Valley, close to the Saskatchewan border, is one of the province's more developed grain elevator interpretation centres. Built in 1929, shortly after the CPR had extended its line, it became one of six elevators in Paradise Valley, even though its population remained modest. The elevator, the last survivor in the village, was acquired by the Paradise Valley and District Museum Society in 1989 and opened to the public in 1995. The concept is a "climb through time" museum with scenes that depict various aspects of prairie life. The displays appear along a sloping stair that makes its way up the grain annex. Today, the attraction hosts more than three thousand visitors a year. A small Canadian Pacific portable-style station rounds out this historic complex.

Pincher Creek

Heritage Acres Farm is a pioneer village run by the Oldman River Antique Equipment and Threshing Club, with old cars, a model railway, a log building, and a variety of historic buildings. Among them is one of the province's oldest grain elevators, which was built in Brocket in 1906 by the United Grain Growers and relocated to this site. Now fully restored and operational, it gives visitors a rare glimpse into how these vanishing landmarks operated.

The Radway Elevator

Completed in 1928 in traditional prairie elevator style, the lone surviving grain elevator in the community of Radway used to be of a row of five. This one is unusual in that it never formed part of the great elevator chains or wheat pools that dominated the prairie skyline but rather was a family operation from the start. The structure was erected by W.D. Kraus at the urging of the local Board of Trade and it shared the location with a grist mill. Although the grist mill was removed in 1959, the elevator still stands. It is designated as a provincial heritage resource.

Raley: Alberta's Oldest

While it doesn't appear on any list of heritage properties, the Alberta Pacific Elevator Company elevator may well be the province's oldest. This wooden thirty-five thousand bushel structure was built in 1905, shortly after the CPR completed its line between Stirling and Cardston, and it was one of four that once stood in this tiny hamlet. The tracks are gone (as is most of the village), and the structure is now privately owned.

The Rowley Row

The ghost town of Rowley, Alberta, contains of one of the more complete railway heritage townscapes to be found anywhere on the prairies. In addition to its Canadian Northern station and its ghost town main street, it retains its three-elevator row. This rail line was one of several constructed at the urging of Alberta premier Alexander Rutherford, and it led north from Drumheller, finally opening in 1911. The first elevators had ill luck, the first collapsing due to poor construction and the second burning. Finally, in 1927, the little village could count a row of three owned by the United Grain Growers, the National Grain Growers, and the Searle Elevator Company. The operations changed hands several times until 1989, when the CNR abandoned the tracks. The grain elevators have since been acquired by the Rowley Community Hall Association and in 2010 were designated a Province of Alberta provincial heritage resource.

Although Rowley calls itself a "ghost town," the elevators as well as the station are well-preserved.

St. Albert's Grain Elevators

Although now utterly overwhelmed by Edmonton's sub-urban sprawl, St. Albert's rail roots remain in good shape. Here on the north side, by the former Canadian Northern tracks, stand two surviving grain elevators. Listed on the Alberta Register of Historic Places, the older of the two prairie giants is the Alberta Grain Company grain elevator. It dates from 1907 and remains one of Alberta's oldest.

In 1937 it was enlarged vertically, storing thirty-thousand bushels of grain at a time until 1989, when grain shipments from St. Albert ceased. Adjacent to it is the Alberta Wheat Pool Grain elevator, and both are now restored and operating as grain elevator interpretation centres. Nearby, the town has recreated its Canadian Northern Railway station, the original having been moved to the Alberta Railway Museum north of Edmonton.

Scandia's Elevator and Stock Yard

Scandia was one of those communities that arose as a result of the CPR's vast irrigation project in southeastern Alberta. The town appeared following the 1927 completion of a branch line from Brooks (the site of the Brooks aqueduct national historic site), one of many that followed the completion of the irrigation project. In 1937 the Federal Grain Company added an elevator that was acquired by the AWP after the war, and it closed in 1977, the same year the CPR shut down the line. To help save the heritage building, it was bought by Eastern Irrigation District Historical Park and Museum and now forms part of an elevator interpretation centre. A component of that complex is the rare survival of an early stock yard, the Bow Slope stockyard, reflecting the co-existence of both wheat farming and cattle ranching. The stock yard still contains the fence gate's ramp scale and shelter used to assemble and ship cattle.

Stettler

In 2003, when Stettler's last grain elevator was closed and put up for sale, the Parrish and Heimbecker Elevator Preservation Society purchased the structure for a dollar and began the work of restoring it to a working example of a prairie grain elevator. The elevators were built in 1920 with a feed mill added in the 1940s. A rare survivor here as well is a coal shed. The elevator has been accessible to the public since 2005, and the elevator office is now a coffee shop. In the shadow of the elevator, the heritage trains of the Alberta Prairie Railway steam excursions wait to take aboard their passengers.

The Warner Elevator Row

When the CPR reached Warner in southern Alberta in 1911, the first of the elevators were built. By the 1920s, Warner could claim a row of seven elevators. Gradually, the earlier structures were replaced, and today the ages of the four surviving elevators range from 1913 to 1960. The oldest is the rare square-sided Alberta Farmers' Coop elevator. The next in age is the Alberta Pacific Grain Elevator, built in 1918, while the Alberta Wheat Pool Elevator dates from 1928. The remaining structures appeared during the 1950s. The fact that three of the original seven have been removed in recent years testifies to the regrettable fact that this row is not protected as a heritage feature. Those remaining continue to function as operating grain elevators.

SASKATCHEWAN

At least two Saskatchewan elevators have been relocated to museum grounds. The 1913 SWP elevator from McCabe now rests in the Sukanen Ship Pioneer Village south of Moose Jaw, while 1928 Keatley elevator completes a heritage railway landscape along with a station and steam locomotive in the Western Development Museum at North Battleford. Others have received designation as municipal heritage properties, such as those in Horizon, built 1922; Parkside, 1959; Prongua (Nelson Farms), 1916 or 1922; Truax, 1964; and Val Marie, 1926. Two of the province's oldest appear to have no designation of heritage recognition of any kind. These are the 1906 Saskatchewan Wheat Pool (SWP) elevator in Creelman and the 1904 elevator in Sintaluta, which now serves as a seed cleaning plant. Throughout the province, a number of small hamlets and even ghost towns may display a single sentinel where once a row has stood. Some remain operational, others sit abandoned and withered. Few are preserved.

Early elevators such as these in an early view of Davidson, Saskatchewan, have vanished from the prairie landscape.

Edam Elevator

In this small prairie town north of The Battlefords lies one of the few examples of a preserved Saskatchewan grain elevator. This former SWP structure, built in 1916, opened in 2005 as the Henry Washbrook Museum, where the first three floors offer displays of First Nations and local area history. The CNo station still faces the elevator from the across the rail line.

Elbow

Built in 1913, this historic grain elevator, the last in this lakeside town, is proposed to move to become a museum.

Hepburn's Museum of Wheat

To date, the 1926 SWP elevator in Hepburn can claim to be that province's only interpretive grain elevator museum. While most of the original equipment remains in place, the building contains a variety of interesting heritage features. The calendar room displays SWP calendars dating from 1933, while the model room shows a model town and railway layout with a miniature grain elevator and station. The museum is run by a band of dedicated volunteers, determined to prevent their heritage icon from suffering the fate of most of the others. A tour of the facility can be topped off by tea in the Ladies Auxiliary tea and craft room. The long-abandoned railway road bed has now been obliterated by new housing developments, as this dormitory community lies only a half hour's commute to Saskatoon.

The Hepburn elevator survives as the Museum of Wheat, where visitors can view the original inner workings.

MANITOBA

Austin, the Homesteaders Village

The Western Canada Flour Mills Company elevator was built in 1905 in Austin on the CPR line and is one of the province's oldest elevators. One of ninety-six mills owned by this company, it was sold to the Manitoba Wheat Pool in 1936, at a time when Western Canada Flour Mills was bankrupt. It now rests on the grounds of the Manitoba Agricultural Museum in Austin.

The Inglis Row

In 1922 the CPR finally laid its tracks north from Russell to Inglis. The town was surveyed and a row of grain elevators built. This row of elevators, four of them constructed in 1922, is said to be the last such row in Canada, although a four-elevator row still survives in Warner, Alberta. While some were owned by the large elevator companies, others were built by local farm coops. All retain their original workings. The Inglis Elevator Heritage Committee acquired the row in 1995, rescuing the aging structures from almost certain demolition. The following year, the Government of Canada rewarded that initiative by declaring the entire row a National Historic Site.

The northern-most of the row is the Patterson elevator, built in 1922 and the only one in the row with a dust collector. Its office building, added in 1951, is the administrative centre for the site. Although the next two elevators in the row are known as the Reliance elevators, they have in fact changed hands over the years, before ending up with the United Grain Growers in 1971. The next in line is the National elevator, still bearing its original name and paint scheme, although it, too, eventually became a Patterson property. The final elevator in the row was built in 1925 by the United Grain Growers. As one of the more significant railway heritage features on the prairies, the site offers both guided and self-guided tours, as well as a small gift shop. Inglis lies north of the Trans-Canada Highway Yellowhead route, north of Russell, Manitoba. (Russell has a preserved elevator of its own, one which marks the western trail head of the Rossburn Subdivision Rail Trail).

Plum Coulee

Although at 1975, the Manitoba Wheat Pool elevator is not old, it is the last of the wooden grain elevators in the Pembina Valley region of Manitoba. In 2001 the Plum Coulee Community Foundation acquired the thirty-five-metre structure and in 2007 opened it as an interpretive centre called the Prairie View Elevator.

Warren

In 2002, when Agricore indicated its intent to demolish its 1948 grain elevator and 1958 annex in Warren, the West Interlake Trading Company leapt into action and acquired the building. In 2005 the group of volunteers set

Now a national historic site, the Inglis, Manitoba, elevator row offers tours of what is said to be the last on the Prairies.

to work preparing the building to become an interpretive centre. The building remains solid, thanks to its sound construction and careful maintenance over the years, and much of the equipment remains in place. Known today as the "Sentinel Grain Elevator," the building is open for tours, and is the terminus for the Prairie Dog Central Railway tour train excursions.

While prairie "sentinels" yet dot the skyline, they are a dying breed. With the demise of the Canada Wheat Board, their numbers will diminish even further. The few that still stand, especially those being preserved, are a valuable celebration of the railway heritage of the prairie provinces.

Chapter Six

The House of Steam: The Railway Roundhouses

If any railway building is scarcer than a station, it is the railway roundhouse. Every divisional point would have one, for these were the all-important engine repair shops. Steam engines required considerable care, such as greasing, oiling, cleaning the flues, and especially for cleaning alkali from the boilers. More semi-circular than round, these buildings would consist a series of stalls whose doors would open toward a turntable. The engine would enter onto the turntable, which would then be turned toward whichever stall was available or appropriate. Inside the roundhouse, large pits sat beneath the engines, and it was here that important repairs took place. The busier the route, the more stalls were needed. Some might contain as many as four dozen, others as few as four.

As the days of steam locomotives began to fade through the 1950s and 60s, roundhouses closed their doors for good. Being large and singularly shaped, they were seldom adaptable to other uses. And taking up valuable space in the yards, most were quickly demolished. A few of those that survive have been carefully preserved.

Toronto's John Street thirty-two-stall roundhouse, a solid brick structure built by the CPR in 1929, has morphed into a brewpub, a furniture store, and a railway museum operated by the Toronto Railway Historical Association. The West Coast Railway Heritage Park in Squamish, British Columbia, keeps much of its historical rolling stock, including the legendary Royal Hudson steam locomotive, in the former CN roundhouse. In Vancouver, the CPR's historic thirty-three-bay roundhouse was rescued from destruction and became a popular focus for Expo 86, and again after considerable efforts by local heritage lovers, it still survives and now contains a display of CPR engine *374*, the first to bring a passenger train into Vancouver, in 1887. In Victoria, the 1913 Esquimaux and Nanaimo roundhouse is now a National Historic Site and will be preserved in a major redevelopment of the former rail yards. By contrast, in what should be considered more enlightened times, in 2007 the town of Kentville demolished Nova Scotia's last railway roundhouse.

Unusual as it may seem, a few new roundhouses have appeared. Calgary's Heritage Park constructed a fully functional roundhouse within the park to maintain its fleet of historic steam locomotives. The Three Valley Gap tourist attraction in British Columbia has added a covered roundhouse to its collection of ghost town buildings. Contents of the roundhouse include a 1929 coach, a 1908 business car, and a 0-4-0 steam engine.

Within the prairie provinces, survivors are rare, and the few that linger are holding on to a precarious existence. Yet there is hope.

Biggar, Saskatchewan

While the Biggar GTP station rots, the roundhouse may enjoy a more positive fate. Built in 1909 with eighteen stalls, it was capable of servicing twenty-one steam locomotives. More than a million bricks were used in its construction, in addition to twelve-metre high fir beams. Tunnels were also discovered that lead to the station. Inside, employee names can be seen carved into the bricks, as well as damage caused to the walls when two runaway engines crashed into them. After its closure in 1960, with steam engines having been replaced by diesel, the roundhouse was leased as a turkey farm, although with the stipulation that it eventually be removed.

In 2007, however, the residents of Biggar and the surrounding area sent a 2,500-name petition to Ottawa to have the structure declared a National Historic Site. They gained support the following year when the Heritage Canada Foundation prioritized it as being one of Canada's top threatened heritage buildings and the

Once commonplace in railway divisional yards, there are few survivors amongst roundhouses. That found in Hanna, Alberta, is a rare exception.

last Grand Trunk roundhouse to survive in the country. Although the grounds have become overgrown, as of 2011 the structure has remained sound. One of the proposed re-uses would be as a museum. In fact, supporters of the proposal have already amassed a number of railway artifacts for such a facility.

Hanna, Alberta

Hanna also possesses a rare roundhouse, which is proposed for private restoration and redevelopment. The turntable remains in place and the wooden doors of the stalls complete the heritage ambience of this heritage railway treasure. The roundhouse was first built with ten stalls in 1913, with another five added in 1920. But the new diesel locomotives proved too large for the early roundhouses, and in 1961 the Hanna roundhouse was closed. It served for a time as an auction house but then fell vacant and was heavily vandalized.

Big Valley

While little more than ruins remain to mark this once-vital roundhouse, it is the only such site to date to have been preserved and interpreted. In 1910 the CNo designated Big Valley to be the line's divisional point between Drumheller and Vegreville. Although operated by the CNo, the line was financed by the Alberta government and was known as the Alberta Midland Railway. The railway erected its standard class-2 divisional station and added a five-stall roundhouse. Closed in the 1920s when the divisional point was relocated to Morrin, the roundhouse site today consists of the walls of the structure along with the remains of the turntable. Self-guiding interpretive signs demarcate a trail through the roundhouse site. Now a designated heritage property, the roundhouse is also part of true railway landscape that includes a grain elevator, baggage car, and the CNo's class-2 divisional station. That landscape comes even more alive when the steam engine of the Stettler tour train puffs to a halt at the station.

The Reston Manitoba Engine House

In 1908, when the CPR extended its line from Reston Manitoba to Wolesley in Saskatchewan, it chose Reston as its eastern terminal. Here, the railway built a station, section house, water tower, coal dock, yards, and elevators. It also added a fan-shaped four-stall engine house with a turntable. No longer needed, the engine house was sold in 1930 to a private business, and it is still in use. The wooden doors denote the four stalls, while the turntable pit, although filled in, is still visible. Not so the remainder of the town's railway heritage, for the rails were lifted in 1960 and the station and elevators removed. The Reston engine house, the last of its kind in Manitoba, was designated as a municipal heritage structure in 1996.

Prince Albert

While not open to tourists, the roundhouse in the northern Saskatchewan city of Prince Albert is one of only two remaining operational roundhouses in Canada. (The other is in Cranbrook.) Built in 1955 by the CNR, today it provides engine repair and maintenance facilities for Omnitrax, which still operates the Prince Albert line.

Visits can be arranged through Omnitrax. The round-house lies east of the Prince Albert station and can be distantly viewed from the street.

Calgary Heritage Park

In 1980 Calgary Heritage Park constructed a fully func-tioning roundhouse to maintain and repair its grow-ing stock of heritage steam locomotives. Based on the CPR's standard number five roundhouse plan, the six-stall facility has been in use since 1981. The turntable, however, dates back to 1907 and first operated in North Bend, British Columbia, and later in Sicamous, from where it was moved to the Heritage Park in 1981.

Chapter Seven

Watering the Steam Engines: The Water Towers

Another railway fixture that is scarcer than railway stations is the railway water tower. Because most steam engines had a limited capacity for the water they needed to carry, anywhere from two thousand to eleven thousand gallons, the railways placed water towers at sufficient intervals for the trains, usually at every other station siding, or thirty to forty kilometres apart. Smaller engines usually could not go beyond eighty kilometres before filling up. Because even the largest towers held no more than 180,000 litres, there needed to be enough water close by to keep the towers full.

The most common style of water tower was the wooden octagonal tower, a few of which still survive. The next most common was the steel tower. Both types needed a source of warmth inside to keep the water from freezing, usually in the form of a stove. To determine how much water remained in the tank, a float that supported a rod that extended through roof and had a ball on top was used, giving a visual from the outside as to what remained. With the building of larger steam locomotives after 1920, with their larger capacities, fewer water towers were needed. Finally, the era of the diesel engine eliminated the need for them at all, and most were demolished, generally unfit for re-use. Where they do survive, they form a rare component of the Prairies' railway heritage

At the Alberta Railway Museum, visitors can explore the interior workings of a rare surviving water tower.

Alberta

HEINSBURG

Located in eastern Alberta, the water tower in the "ghost town" of Heinsburg was built by the CNR in 1928 in what was the branch line's eastern terminus. The tower has been restored by members of the community, as has the CN station. Both remain on their original sites.

NEW BRIGDEN

Built by the Canadian National Railway in 1925, the New Brigden water tower was, like the others, an engineering marvel. Constructed entirely of wood and covered with shipslab siding, the tower is the tallest structure in this small village, at thirteen metres high. Like other similar water towers, the water level inside could be read by means of a float. To prevent the water from freezing, the inner tank rested on twelve vertical timbers about 5.5 metres above the ground and was heated by a stove. While tracks and station are both gone, the New Brigden tower alone celebrates the community's railway heritage. It was designated in 2009 as a municipal heritage resource.

Other surviving towers in Alberta include steel towers beside the site of the Bassano station, and, in the Humboldt yard, the 1919 wooden water tower from Gibbons, which is now in the Alberta Railway Museum north of Edmonton. There is also the GTP's Delburne water tower, which moved to the Anthony Henday Museum beside the former GTP station.

Manitoba

GLENBORO CPR WATER TOWER

Just as the railway company had standard designs for their stations, so too did they have "plans" for their water towers, and those in Glenboro and Clearwater went by "Plan 1." They were among seventy-five such towers built along the CPR lines throughout Manitoba. Although they have been out of use for decades, ever since the CPR and other railways converted their locomotives from coal to diesel, they were designated as provincial heritage sites in 1993. The Glenboro tower was then owned by the town but sadly torched by arsonists in April 2008.

CLEARWATER CPR WATER TOWER

The water tower in Clearwater Manitoba is identical in style and age to that which stood in Glenboro. Like the Glenboro tower, it was designated as a provincial heritage structure. This 180,000-litre tower still retains its motor and pump, which were used to prevent the water from freezing. It is owned by its local municipality of Louise.

WINNIPEG BEACH

The railways realized that with the natural riches along their lines, such as the Rocky Mountains, they could profit from recreation. In 1910 the CPR acquired sixty hectares of land on Lake Winnipeg and established a resort complex of accommodations as well as recreational and amusement facilities. To provide water to its resort and for its steam locomotives, in 1928 it constructed a steel water tower that was forty metres high and had a ninety-thousand-litre capacity. On busy summer weekends, as many as forty thousand excursionists would crowd onto the trains for the sixty-five-kilometre run from Winnipeg to the popular amusement park. But in 1964, the park closed and the water tower fell into disuse. Today, it still stands and is a designated heritage landmark. With its steel tank resting atop the four steel legs, it is the only one of five original such structures surviving in Manitoba.

Many water towers have made their way into museums across the prairies. The tower from McCreary, a standard wooden structure with a 180,000-litre capacity, rests on the grounds of the Manitoba Agricultural Museum in Austin. A steel water tower still stands by the tracks in Carberry.

Saskatchewan

GLASLYN

Perhaps the reason that the 1926 CN water tower in Glaslyn had remained in such good condition is that it continued to supply water to the town until 1993, when a new municipal water tower began operation. Today, the preserved tower, along with the CN station, is part of the Glaslyn Museum and forms one of the truest railway landscapes on the prairies.

The water tower and station at the Alberta Railway Museum offer a glimpse of a vanished landscape.

HAGUE

In 1903 the CNo extended its tracks through Hague, Saskatchewan, and built one of its many water towers. Unlike the usual tapered towers favoured by the CPR, that at Hague is vertical. The overall structure extends eight metres high and could contain the usual 180,000 litres of water. The inner tub, which contained the water, is made of three-inch cedar and supported by five-metre-long square timbers and extends seven metres high. Now repainted a bright red, it still rests by track and is a proud visual symbol of this railway community.

HARRIS

Built by the CN in 1934, the Harris water tower, like many railway buildings, had a plan number, that being 150-99, one of only nine built in Saskatchewan. The eight-sided tower could contain 180,000 litres. During the days of steam, an estimated five hundred such water towers once dotted the prairie landscape. Threatened with the emergence of diesel power, the Harris water tower was relocated. With much of its interior workings intact, the structure is now a municipal heritage site. It is located beside the Harris and District Museum on Railway Avenue near Highway 7. A CN caboose also stands on the site.

At Glaslyn, Saskatchewan, the CN station and railway water tower have been preserved on their original sites.

KENASTON

It is always refreshing to witness a small community undertake the restoration of a scarce railway feature. In 2009 the town of Kenaston completed the restoration of its 1910 CNo water tower. This typical structure was constructed of wood, tapered, and capable of containing 180,000 litres of water for the steam locomotives. The restoration involved a new foundation, repairs to the exterior, and repainting the tower its original tuscan red and cream colours. It is now a tourist attraction on the Louis Riel Trail tourism corridor and is one of only five such towers in that province, three which remain on-site.

Chapter Eight

Bridging the Prairies: The Railway Bridges

While the railway companies building across the prairie provinces were spared the unrelenting muskeg of northern Ontario and the death-defying gorges of the western mountains, they did encounter some of Canada's most challenging bridge crossings. The CPR, of course, was the first to cross the vast plains and it encountered relatively few crossings west of Winnipeg. Its first bridge structures were timber trestles, easily accommodating the earliest trains, which were relatively short and the engines light.

The earliest type of bridge was known as the Howe truss bridge, a design created by William Howe as early as 1840. The earliest bridges used either the truss or the timber pile technique, and almost all were constructed of wood. But as the wood supply dwindled, and trains became heavier, steel deck plate girders replaced wood as the material of choice, while the supports were usually of poured concrete. Many of the prairies bridges are now designated as heritage properties. Indeed, the Province of Saskatchewan has completed studies on fifteen potential heritage railway bridges.

A relatively short bridge at Boharm, Saskatchewan, for example, while only six metres long, was built in 1907 and is a very early example of a steel I-beam bridge. The 1917 bridge at Kamsack, Saskatchewan, while only fifty metres long, is an early example of a through truss bridge. A 110-metre timber bridge still crosses the Cutknife river near Gallivan.

One of the CPR's earliest bridges was built in 1893, and it crosses the Souris River between Pasqua and North Portal. At only fifty metres long, it is one of the Prairies' oldest bridges. Other smaller heritage spans include bridges in Regina, Tantallon, and Swift Current. It is, however, the massive bridges that inspire the most awe, resembling delicate spiders' webs, high above the wide valleys, but sturdy enough to support the heaviest of freight trains.

In Saskatchewan alone, more than sixty railway bridges exceed two hundred metres in length. In fact, that province can count more than 1,900 railway bridges.[11]

Alberta

EDMONTON'S HIGH LEVEL BRIDGE

Now one of Edmonton's iconic landmarks, the famous High Level Bridge offers passage for both rail and road traffic. At nearly 780 metres long and soaring forty-eight metres above the waters of the North Saskatchewan River, it is said to rank among the four greatest trestles constructed during the early days of the CPR. From 1913 until 1989, using the upper deck, some twenty metres above the lower deck, CPR trains regularly crossed the bridge. In fact, three sets of tracks crossed the bridge, with the centre track for the CPR trains and the two outer tracks for the Edmonton streetcars.

Unlike usual, the streetcars would travel on the left track rather than the right. Should the streetcar have become disabled while stranded precariously above the river, passengers would thereby be able to disembark from the doors on the right hand side of the streetcar and onto the centre of the bridge.

Streetcar service ended in September 1951, while the CPR ceased using the bridge in 1995. Shortly after that, the Edmonton Radial Railway Society (ERRS) began to install poles and overhead wires and in 1997 inaugurated a tour tram over the bridge. After operating a restored Japanese streetcar and a German streetcar, in 2011 the ERRS brought back into operation Edmonton Streetcar #3, restored to its original 1912 condition. The ERRS also operates a small museum in the Streetcar Barn in Strathcona, as well as a fleet in Fort Edmonton Park, where its workshops are located.

EDMONTON'S LOW LEVEL BRIDGE

Now used for vehicles only, this structure was built by the CNo in order to link South Edmonton or Strathcona with Edmonton proper by rail. It opened in 1902 with a length of 212 metres on three steel truss spans. The tracks were gone by 1948.

THE BEVERLEY BRIDGE, EDMONTON

Travellers entering Edmonton from the east on the northern Trans-Canada Highway will be impressed by the railway bridge over the North Saskatchewan a short distance to their north. Built by the GTP to bring their express Winnipeg to Edmonton trains over the river, it opened in 1908. With a length of over five hundred metres it rose only twelve metres above the river. Workers travelling between the communities of Clover Bar and Beverley would walk across the bridge, using

the intermittent water barrels beside the tracks should a train approach. While it was originally constructed to accommodate vehicles as well, today it carries only trains and is the CN's main line as well as the route used by VIA Rail.

THE MILL CREEK BRIDGE, EDMONTON

Although it is neither grand nor distinctive, the all-wooden Mill Creek trestle represents the historic route of the Edmonton, Yukon and Pacific Railway, which was chartered in 1902 in order to finally link Edmonton with Strathcona, which were on opposite sides of the North Saskatchewan River. Despite protests from Edmonton, the CPR had refused to build a connection over the river and into Edmonton from its terminus in Strathcona. The EY&P was chartered to correct that by crossing the new Low Level bridge, which had been built by the government. While the Low Level Bridge represented the river crossing itself, the Mill Creek trestle represents a little-altered example of one the prairie's oldest wooden trestles. Today it forms part of a trailway that follows the railway roadbed through the Mill Creek Ravine.

RED DEER'S CPR BRIDGE

Now part of the popular Waskasoo Trail system in Red Deer Alberta, the CPR's bridge over the Red Deer River is a landmark located in this one-time railway divisional town. The steel truss bridge was built in 1908 in anticipation of the Alberta Central Railway completing a line from Coal Banks to Rocky Mountain House. However, funding fell short and the line was taken over by the CPR in 1911, and it established a divisional point in the community. Built as a double span steel truss bridge, it also displays a wooden trestle at the south end. Rail traffic continued to rumble across the bridge until 1991, when, as part of Red Deer's downtown redevelopment, the CPR moved its track alignment west of the city centre, allowing the conversion of the bridge for pedestrian use.

Looking oddly out of place today, a concrete pillar stands beside Taylor Drive in Red Deer. A plaque beside it recounts that it is all that remains of a bridge built by the Alberta Central Railway in 1911 to cross the CPR tracks. When the CPR assumed control of the ACR, it decided to no longer use this bridge, and the structure was later removed. Taylor Drive itself occupies the former rail bed of the CPR, where, until the late 1990s, when the tracks were removed to construct Taylor Drive, a second pillar also stood.

THE MINTLAW BRIDGE, RED DEER

Once the largest bridge in Alberta, the Mintlaw bridge is located on the abandoned CPR line south of Red Deer. The Alberta Central Railway began construction in 1910 but was bankrupt before it could complete the structure. The CPR took over the line and finished the bridge in 1912. At that point, the massive bridge stretched nearly a kilometre long and rose thirty metres above the river, its spans resting on fifteen piers. Abandoned by the railway in 1981, the bridge is now owned by Red Deer County and is being considered for pedestrian use on a trail that would link Forth Junction with Sylvan Lake. The structure lies south of Red Deer, but is not easily seen from any public vantage point.

ARDLEY'S TRESTLE

Another Red Deer area bridge was that built by the GTP over the Red Deer River in 1911. It measured five hundred metres long and fifty-five metres high. At first it was a wooden trestle bridge, but when it was destroyed by flooding a few years later, the centre portion was replaced with two steel spans. After being taken out again in 1952, this time by ice, it was replaced entirely by a steel trestle. It remains in use. The structure lies east of Secondary Highway 921, although there is no public vantage point from which to easily view this mighty structure.

THE OLDMAN BRIDGE, LETHBRIDGE

One of the most historic of Canada's railway bridges, and one of the most photographed, is the CPR's high level trestle over the Oldman River in Lethbridge. When it was completed in 1909, it was the highest of its kind in the world and to this day remains the longest. Its twenty-two girder spans and single truss span cover a distance of more than 1.25 kilometres and rise nearly one hundred metres above the river. The engineer who designed it was John Schwitzer, who also designed the Monarch trestle to the west of Lethbridge and the famous CPR spiral tunnels in the Rocky Mountain chain.

The bridge helped to eliminate an earlier, more circuitous route by replacing twenty-two smaller bridges and thirty-seven curves. It reduced the distance between Lethbridge and Fort MacLeod by eight kilometres. More than 645 railcars were needed to ship the girders from the Canada Bridge Company in Windsor to the Oldman River valley. A special design feature was the trough girders, which would keep a train from falling off the bridge should it derail. Because of its popularity with photographers and visitors, the City of Lethbridge has created a lookout point and installed interpretive signage. Nearby are walkways and plaques describing Lethbridge's early coal mining story. Fort Whoop-up Historic Park lies at the base of the bridge.

The CPR bridge over the Oldman River at Lethbridge was described as an engineering marvel and is one of the largest in North America.

THE MONARCH TRESTLE, MONARCH

Around the same time as the CPR crews were bridging the Oldman River at Lethbridge, they were also hard at work west of Monarch building an almost equally impressive steel trestle over the same river. When finished in 1908, it stood more than six hundred metres long. The Monarch station, closed around the 1960s, is now a dwelling within the town. The Monarch bridge is about six kilometres west of Monarch but, unlike its counterpart in Lethbridge, twenty kilometres to the east, it lacks a viewing point.

THE BRIDGES OF THE ROSEBUD VALLEY, DRUMHELLER

The Rosebud River and Serviceberry Creek have eroded spectacular valleys, creating the layered badlands for which the Drumheller area is world famous. This valley proved to be the only viable route along which the CNo could build their line between Drumheller and Calgary. While none of the bridges along it are monumental, the countless twists and turns of the rivers meant that the railway, operating here as the Alberta Midland Railway (in reality a part of the CNo system), needed to bridge the little waterways sixty-two times within fifty kilometres. The line was built initially to haul the coal from the many coal mines near

Drumheller. The ghost town of Wayne, about 10 kilometres east of Drumheller on Highway 10X, is located near the eastern section of this line, which remains in use, although it is limited today to carrying grain.

EAST COULEE'S WOODEN BRIDGE

East of the Rosebud River, along the Red Deer River, the rail line lies abandoned. Among the many abandoned

A rare surviving wooden truss bridge that once served the Atlas coal mine east of Drumheller.

mine sites, the historic Atlas mine, which retains many of its structures and rail cars, is now a National Historic Site. A rare wooden truss bridge crosses the Red Deer River just west of the mine. The structure built by the CNR in 1948 consists of six wooden truss spans resting on concrete piers. Tracks still sit between the wooden planks. Although the Atlas Coal Mine has become a tourist attraction, the bridge sits neglected. The much-photographed ghost town of Dorothy, with its ancient grain elevator and early churches, lies east of the Atlas mine. The mine and bridge are on Highway 10 about twenty kilometres east of Drumheller.

ROCHFORT BRIDGE, MAYERTHORPE

One of North America's longest wooden trestles, the Rochfort Bridge, near Mayerthorpe, Alberta, stretches more than eight hundred metres long across the Paddle River. After the CNo completed the bridge in 1914, farmers would herd their cattle across the structure, while pedestrians caught before an oncoming train would simply wait on one of the barrel stands located beside the tracks. Braver souls have been known to enjoy the thrill of driving their car over the mighty structure.

In 1935 soil slippage in the valley forced the pilings four metres out of line, requiring new pilings down to bedrock. In 1944 pressure from unusually severe ice floes once more forced the bridge out of line. Later, in 1956, fire damaged more than two hundred metres of the bridge's timber supports, once again halting traffic on the CNR's busy Edmonton to Whitecourt line. It remains in use today, although trains must limit their speed to fourteen kilometres per hour.

A lookout area on Range Road 80 south of Highway 43, a short distance east of the village of Rochfort, allows spectators to view trains crossing the mighty structure.

The popularity of the trestle has influenced at least one business — the Rochfort Bridge Trading Post — to include the "Bridge Burger Challenge" on its menu.

The Sangudo trestle, another significant bridge, lies nearby on the west end of the village of Sangudo, a few kilometres to the east of Rochfort Bridge. Although smaller, it is nonetheless an impressive feat of engineering and is best viewed from Range Road 7, south of Highway 43, or from the Riverside Campground and Day Use Area in the village itself.

THE ENTWHISTLE CONNECTION

One of western Alberta's most spectacular gorges is that which was carved by the Pembina River following the last Ice Age. By 1908 the Grand Trunk Pacific Railway had constructed its main line up to the brink of the gorge and halted there long enough for the community on the east side of the gorge to become a busy end of steel known as Entwhistle. At sixty metres deep and 350 metres wide, the chasm proved a sufficient obstacle for the GTP, and it spent two years bridging that gaping abyss. Finally, in 1910, the trains began to cross the dizzying trestle, and the tiny mining town of Evansburg, on the opposite side, began to take shape. Still in use today, the Entwhistle trestle is one of Canada's highest.

BLINDMAN RIVER BRIDGE, BLACKFALDS

In 1911 the Canada Northwestern Railway built a long wooden trestle that stretched six hundred metres across the Blindman River near the community of Blackfalds, now part of the growing Red Deer urban area. While the end portions retain their wooden piers, the central section now consists of steel girders. Because much of the old trestle was filled in, the bridge has been shortened to about two hundred metres. The CNR continues to run their freight trains over the structure.

BRIGGS RAVINE

A rare timber trestle bridge, one of the last in the region, the Briggs bridge crosses a ravine near the Blindman River east of the vanished village of Briggs, and not far to the west of Blackfalds. It stretches more than two hundred metres across the gully. It was constructed by the Canada Northwestern Railway, now the CNR. Unfortunately, the trestle, about three kilometres north of Highway 11A, is not close to any public vantage point.

WASKATENAU'S WOODEN TRESTLE

In 1919 the St. Paul de Metis Railway, part of the CNo system, was opened between Heinsburg and Waskatenau. The aim was to serve the settlements east of Edmonton and north of the North Saskatchewan River. At Waskatenau it crossed the creek of the same name. Here, a long wooden trestle was erected and dam built to provide water for the steam locomotives. Once the railways began to switch to diesel from steam, the dam was removed, and much of the wooden trestle filled with earth. It nonetheless remains very much a heritage feature, as well as being the western terminus of the Iron Horse Trail.

East of Waskatenau, the Iron Horse Trail passes through the quiet village of Bellis, which once could claim a class-3 CNo station (added by the CNR) and yet another extensive low-level trestle. West of Waskatenau, the still active rails cross the Sturgeon River near Gibbons station on a timber trestle bridge, which is seven hundred metres long and soars thirty metres above the river.

THE BEAVER RIVER BRIDGE, COLD LAKE

Now part of the popular Iron Horse Trail, this large bridge that crosses the Beaver River south of Cold Lake Alberta consists of a single steel truss span resting on two concrete piers, with wooden frames on each end. Nearly five hundred metres long and almost sixty-five metres high, it was abandoned by the CNR in 1999.

Saskatchewan

SASKATOON'S BRIDGES

In 1908 the Canadian Bridge Company of Walkerville, Ontario, built for the Canadian Northern Railway a five-hundred-metre bridge over the South Saskatchewan River, a link that was vital in connecting Winnipeg with Edmonton. The company later became part of the CNR. To complete its link from Wynyard to Saskatoon, the CPR added a bridge over the river in the same year. This four-hundred-metre-long high level bridge, known as the Macdonald Bridge, today includes a foot bridge that is popular with walkers and joggers alike. Like many of the other walking bridges of the Prairies, this one is not for the vertiginously faint of heart. This structure lies along Spadina Crescent East, near the intersection of 33rd Street, where a parking lot by the river offers visitors an opportunity to view the bridge or mount the steps to cross it. The University of Saskatchewan sits on the east bank, while the main part of the city is on the west. The current CNR bridge, which has no pedestrian walkway, lies near Spadina Crescent West, some distance south of 11th Street West.

NORTH BATTLEFORD'S BRIDGES

When the CNo was laying its tracks across central Saskatchewan, it opted to remain on the north side of the Battle River, thereby bypassing the older historic settlement and one-time capital of Battleford, which lay on the south bank. Here, the CNo established a divisional point and new community called North Battleford. Later, in

1912, the GTP extended a branch along the south side of the river, linking Swift Current with Battleford, and it erected a 93-span, 220-metre timber trestle over the Battle River. The structure was upgraded in 1924 and again in 1942 with two steel truss spans replacing the old timber spans. The abandoned GTP trestle south of the town beside 2nd Street South was purchased by the Town of Battleford to be incorporated into a trail system. This connects such local attractions as the historic Government House, which dates from Battleford's role as the territorial capital, with the Fort Battle National Historic Site.

A second, longer trestle lies west of the town, where it also crosses the Battle River. Also abandoned, it is not visible from any public vantage point. A third even longer bridge lies to the north of North Battleford and was built by the CNo where it formed a junction with the tracks of the GTP at a location called Battleford Junction. A steel truss bridge more than one thousand metres long, it now carries the CNR main line across the North Saskatchewan River.

PRINCE ALBERT

One of Saskatchewan's more important railway bridges was that built by the Canadian Northern Railway over the North Saskatchewan River in 1909, allowing the CNo to extend its main line from Winnipeg to Edmonton. It consisted of seven steel truss spans and a swinging portion that allowed steamboats to pass. Since the river crossing had until then been by cable ferry, the residents of Prince Albert grew anxious for a more permanent link. In fact, the community went so far as to subsidize the construction of a station and roundhouse if the CNo would expedite the bridge.

Then the province got into the act, calling for the bridge to accommodate vehicular traffic as well. When it opened in 1909, the bridge consisted of five Pratt steel truss spans of fifty metres each and one steel truss swing span of eighty metres. Finally, after 1918, steamers no longer plied the North Saskatchewan, and the swing span was fixed shut. Motor vehicles stopped using the railway bridge in 1960 in favour of the Diefenbaker Bridge. Trains, however, continue to use the old railway bridge

ST. LOUIS'S GTP BRIDGE

This four-hundred-metre-long bridge across the South Saskatchewan River is made up of six steel trusses and was opened in 1915. For several years, local citizens and the provincial government continued to press first the GTP and then the CNR to incorporate a roadway into the bridge, but both companies repeatedly denied the request, even though the original design would in fact allow such additions. Finally, after the province threatened to plank in the bridge for cars, the CNR capitulated and in 1928 added traffic wings to the sides of the bridge. A smaller central lift span was included to allow steamboat traffic to pass beneath, although that form of transportation has long since ceased.

Until the traffic attachments were added, cars were forced to use a ferry service located about three kilometres upstream from the village. The CNR abandoned the line in 1983 and the bridge's two traffic wings continue to carry vehicular traffic. A replacement bridge 1.5 kilometres away is scheduled for completion in 2012, when the old bridge will be closed. Efforts are under way for its preservation.

The town of St. Louis is situated on Highway 2, south of Prince Albert. A small roadside park near the south end of the bridge offers opportunities to photograph the bridge. A large information kiosk outlines the history of the region and the many ferry crossings that once operated along the river.

While the St. Louis "ghost train" no longer crosses the unusual road and rail bridge over the North Saskatchewan River, cars will continue to use it until a new bridge opens nearby.

THE FENTON BRIDGE

In 1906, a few kilometres downstream from St. Louis, the CNo constructed a five-hundred-metre bridge across the South Saskatchewan River. Built first as a timber structure to replace washed out bridges, it was rebuilt in 1982. While the centre portion consists of a steel truss span, the two edges are made of timber pile and frame. It lies on the Hudson Bay Junction to Prince Albert section of the former CNo rail line about twelve kilometres west of the community of Birch Hills. Vehicular traffic must use a privately operated ferry to cross the river. A short side trip down a local road on the north side of the river and west of the ferry will bring the visitor within view of the mighty structure.

MESKANAW'S WOODEN TRESTLE: SASKATCHEWAN'S LONGEST

At more than four hundred metres long, the Meskanaw bridge is the longest wooden trestle bridge remaining in Saskatchewan. It lies beside the highway a short distance west of the village of the same name. The structure was built by the Canadian National Railway in 1929. Although no interpretive sign marks this major engineering feat, a short pullout on the shoulder on Highway 41 west of Melfort permits easy viewing of this daunting structure from just a few metres away.

OUTLOOK'S SKYTRAIL BRIDGE

Now one of Canada's most stunning walking bridges, the CPR bridge in Outlook, Saskatchewan, was, at one thousand metres, the second-longest railway bridge in Canada and its piers the world's highest. The bridge was built as part of a CPR initiative to provide a more direct link between Edmonton and Saint Paul, Minnesota. In addition to the rail crossing, the residents of the area lobbied hard for the bridge to accommodate vehicular traffic by means of a roadway beneath the tracks. But poor communication between the provincial government and

The wooden Meskanaw bridge is the longest such structure in Saskatchewan.

the CPR caused the negotiations to collapse and the CPR built the rail-only bridge.

The remarkable structure consisted of eight spans, which had been shipped from the Lachine Bridge over the St. Lawrence in Montreal, each measuring eighty metres long, as well as a pair of twenty-seven-metre spans. The first trains crossed the structure in 1912 and continued to do so until 1987, when the CPR abandoned the line. In 2005 the bridge was decked in to become the Skytrail Bridge. Now part of the Trans Canada Trail system, it is Canada's longest pedestrian bridge — and not a good idea for those with vertigo. The government later did construct a vehicle bridge to the south of the railway bridge, and now bypassed by a newer bridge, it is also a heritage structure.

NIPAWIN'S "CROOKED" BRIDGE

Built in 1929, the double-decked plate girder bridge over the Saskatchewan River in Nipawin consisted of five steel truss spans resting on four concrete piers. A five-metre-wide roadway is situated on the lower deck. The bridge replaced a small cable ferry that had in turn replaced a precarious cable car, which carried travellers high above the river.

When word of the CPR's proposed bridge became known in 1924, the area residents began to lobby for a vehicular segment to be incorporated. The original site of Nipawin was seven kilometres from where the CPR chose to locate their station, then called Ravine Bank, causing the town, as ever, to move the buildings to trackside. The bridge earned the nickname the "Crooked Bridge" due to the Y configuration required by the cars to approach it. The bridge is over six hundred metres long and consists of fifteen steel spans. A new traffic bridge opened in 1974, giving vehicles a straighter alternative. The CPR line between Nipawin and Choiceland is now

operated by the Torch River Railway, a short line railway, which still uses the historic "crooked" bridge. Nipawin is on Highway 36, north of Tisdale.

THE HEART'S HILL TIMBER BRIDGE

Even small bridges can carry local heritage significance, such as this small timber bridge at Heart's Hill. It was built in 1930 when the CNR extended its branch line from Unity to Bodo in central Saskatchewan. The last structure to survive on this branch, it witnessed its last train in 1993 and then the line was abandoned. It still features its original wooden trusses, piers, timber bents, and stringer spans. Designated as a municipal heritage property in 2006, it is listed on the Saskatchewan Register of Heritage Properties and is a popular local landmark, especially among artists. It is situated northwest of Kerrobert, about thirty kilometres west of the village of Luseland.

Manitoba

WINNIPEG, BRIDGING THE RED AND THE ASSINIBOINE

In a very short period of time, the forks of the Red and Assiniboine rivers became the focus of Canada's east–west rail network. The lines of the CPR, the CNo, the GTP, and the Northern Pacific and Manitoba Railways all converged on the forks. Winnipeg boomed into what many called the Chicago of the north. To carry the tracks of these many lines across the two rivers, several bridges were constructed. In 1914 the Canadian Northern Railway built a lift bridge over the Assiniboine a short distance from its confluence with the Red. No longer in use, the lift bridge is today part of a walking trail along the Red River and leads into The Forks heritage site in

Winnipeg. With its massive concrete counterbalance, it is an attraction for artists to display their works. Adjacent to it, a newer bridge still carries CN and VIA Rail traffic across the Assiniboine.

Further downstream from the Forks, both the CNR and the CPR use massive steel trestle bridges to carry their respective main line traffic, while still further downstream, an abandoned CPR swing bridge marks its once busy North Kildonan crossing with the centre span fixed into the open position. Meanwhile, upstream on the Assiniboine, a four-span steel trestle bridge, also now abandoned, until recent times carried CNR traffic to its Oak Pointe yards.

THE UNO TRESTLE, RIVERS, MANITOBA

This prominent landmark of the otherwise flat landscape around the former railway divisional town of Rivers, Manitoba, crosses the Minnewashta Creek. When built by the Grand Trunk Pacific Railway in 1908, the trestle stretched nearly a kilometre and a half in length. After it took over operations of the GTP, the CNR filled in much of the trestle and replaced the wooden supports with those of steel.

In 1991 the railway closed the bridge for five days while crews converted the massive crossing from an open-deck bridge to a ballast-deck bridge that consisted of solid concrete forms into which ballast could be placed. Today, it is less than a quarter of its original length. The presence of this looming structure has given rise to the name of a local business, the Trestle Greenhouse. While the trestle remains in use, with CN trains crossing it several times a day, as well as VIA Rail's cross-country trains, the vacant heritage station in Rivers lies neglected.

THE PAS, MANITOBA

After the CNo undertook construction of the Hudson Bay Railway, it halted the line on the south bank of the South Saskatchewan River and showed little interest in bridging it. When the Canadian government began completing the Hudson Bay Railway in 1913, they constructed a six-span steel truss bridge across the wide river. While it is one of that province's longest railway bridges, it is a low structure. Its significance lies in its strategic importance in crossing a key barrier to the completion of the line. The bridge continues to carry trains to the grain port of Churchill and to the mining and First Nations communities of northern Manitoba. Rail lovers venture over it on VIA Rail's popular Churchill train to view the polar bears.

THE PORT NELSON GHOST BRIDGE

Perhaps the most unusual of the prairie province bridges is that built at Port Nelson. In 1913 the Canadian government took over the task of completing the Hudson Bay Railway to its terminus at Port Nelson from the CNo. Tracks gradually made their way north of The Pas, reaching the Nelson River in 1914. Duncan William McLaughlin was scarcely a dozen years out of engineering at McGill University in Montreal when he became chief engineer for the construction of the Port Nelson grain terminal. Because of the shallow depth and shifting silts, the only place to construct the wharf was on an island offshore, which necessitated a lengthy bridge.

In 1915 the tenders went out for the construction of the bridge. The successful applicant was the veteran Dominion Bridge Company of Montreal. They began the job of assembling seventeen steel spans of more than thirty-five metres in length each. Throughout the short shipping seasons of 1915 and 1916, the bolts and beams began to arrive, and on August 26, 1916, the last span was hoisted into place. To further reduce the risk of ice and currents, a barge was sunk upstream to break up any ice and the bridge itself was raised higher.

Then, in the summer of 1918, after an expenditure of more than $6 million, all work at Port Nelson ground to halt. But the demand for an ocean grain port for the prairies did not. In 1927, with the western farmers howling for the completion of the railway, a British harbour engineer named Frederick Palmer was hired by the government of William Lyon Mackenzie King to compare the harbours at Port Nelson and Churchill. Harshly criticizing the choice of Port Nelson, he recommended that Churchill become the new grain port. The location would create a longer route but would provide a safer harbour.

In September 1929, the first grain was shipped from Churchill, and Port Nelson settled into obscurity as a ghost town. Ruins of buildings litter the grounds, a beached dredger lies on the shores of the island, but the most prominent ruin of all is the sturdy seventeen-span railway trestle, so solidly built that a train could cross it yet today. Few have visited this remote site, the only ways in being by boat or float plane.[12]

Chapter Nine

The Short Lines

Branch Line Abandonment

If in the early years of railway construction across the prairie provinces there were insufficient rail lines, by the 1930s there were simply too many. The CPR was the first to cross the area and showed little interest in adding many branch lines. The main reason for building the line in the first place, after all, was to fulfill a promise to British Columbia: for joining confederation, the government would finance the construction of a railway to the coast. To encourage the CPR, the government offered the company extensive grants of land as well as a twenty-five year monopoly on shipping grain. This resulted in the expected howls of protest from prairie farmers, and the government approved two more national lines, namely the piecemeal network of Mackenzie and Mann's Canadian Northern Railway and the government-financed Grand Trunk Pacific Railway.

While the CNo happily extended branch lines almost everywhere, the GTP focused more on reaching the coast and added few branch lines of its own. When the First World War ended, and with it the financial future of the CNo and GTP, the Canadian National Railway was created to take over the bankrupt lines. With access to public funds, the new CNR had little restraint when it came to branch line construction, and to compete, the CPR followed suit. And so, from nine thousand kilometres of tracks in 1906, more than three times that amount was in place by 1935: twenty-six thousand kilometres

But the times conspired against so many branch lines. One factor was the Crow's Nest Pass freight rates, by which the railways were required to reduce the shipping rates they charged the farmers. As a result, by the mid-30s, the railway companies were losing money. Truck companies offered better rates and more flexibility. This meant that the railways could no longer afford to subsidize the lightly used branch lines from the profits of their main lines.

Until 1975 the government had helped to subsidize these money-losing routes, but the Hall Commission recommended closing the costliest of the lines, and finally, in 1995, most restrictions on branch line abandonments were lifted. In just five years, more than two thousand kilometres of branch lines were gone, along with most of the grain elevators that lined them. Elevator villages turned into ghost towns by the dozens.

Responding to the plight and hardships that befell the smaller farmers as a result of those abandonments, some of the branch lines have sprung back to life. In 1989 the Government of Saskatchewan enacted legislation that allowed the chartering and financial assisting of locally operated short lines on the branches being proposed for abandonment by the major railway companies.

THE ST. LOUIS GHOST TRAIN

Some abandoned rail lines, it seems, don't want to stay abandoned. Such would be the case of the "Ghost Train" of St. Louis, Saskatchewan. St. Louis is a small one-time railway village perched on the North Saskatchewan River. Although its rails have been lifted since 1983, many residents and visitors claim that hasn't stopped the trains.

The strange story of a ghost train has been told many times. The site where it occurs is a former railway crossing along a side road around eight kilometres north of the town. Those who have witnessed the phenomenon claim that, far down the track, they see a single headlight, similar to those of old steam locomotives. It seems to keep getting closer but then vanishes. Often a smaller red light is seen with it.

The legend has it that a conductor was decapitated while checking the tracks and that the red light is the lantern the conductor was using to find his missing head. A pair of high school students, as part of a school project, launched an investigation of the light's cause. Drawing a straight line down the track from their position at the crossing on a topographical map, they asked one of their fathers to position his car at various locations along the projection and flash his headlights while the trio communicated by cell phone. Finally, one the locations showed that indeed the phantom light could be nothing more than approaching car headlights enhanced by ground-level refraction.

Most believers, however, dismiss that theory, and still attribute the lights to something that cannot be so easily explained. In fact, a local café calls itself the Phantom Light Café. A visit to the crossing in 2011 revealed that the old railway right of way had become so overgrown that distant headlights would not easily penetrate the growth.

THE SHORT LINE REVIVAL

Just when it seemed as if the branch lines were doomed in Canada, various provincial governments have made it easier for short lines to operate on those branch lines. Some are farmers' co-ops, others may be subsidiaries of larger rail lines.

The Burlington Northern Santa Fe

This very short line operates only within the city of Winnipeg, yet its roots go back to 1903. It began as the Midland Railway of Manitoba, but ended up merging with the large American railway the Burlington Northern. Today, it is based in the city of Winnipeg, where its two-stall engine house sits north of Taylor Street, housing its solitary locomotive and a caboose. The line hauls processed corn, steel, and construction materials to its links with the CN at their Fort Rouge yards or the CPR at their Logan Street yards.

Keewatin Railway Company (KRC)

When the Hudson Bay Railway in 2003 announced its closure of the Sherridan Rail line, which had served the Leaf Lake mine, the three First Nation communities that would be most severely affected signed a joint memorandum of understanding: Tataskweyak Cree Nation, Mathias Colomb Cree Nation, and War Lake First Nation bought up the line in 2004. Headquartered in The Pas, the KRC operates mixed trains twice weekly between The Pas and Pukatawagan, a distance of some 250 kilometres. This is the only short line in the Prairies to carry both passengers and freight.

Boundary Trail Railway

In 2009, producers along a twenty-five kilometre CP branch line formed the Boundary Trail Railway Company to ship produce from along the line and save the many small communities from severe economic decline. It is the first such short line in Manitoba, although similar lines had been operating in Saskatchewan for a number of years. Its thirty-six-kilometre route extends from Binney Siding to almost Manitou, and the company owns a further eighty kilometres from Binney Siding to almost Killarney. In its first year alone, the Boundary Trail Railway shipped five hundred carloads of grain.

The Central Manitoba Railway (CMR)

This short line operation runs on two former branch lines: one from Beach Junction in Winnipeg to Pine Falls, about ninety-five kilometres; and the other from Carmen to Graysville, a distance of eighty kilometres. The CMR acquired the two subdivisions from the CNR in 1999, and today its four locomotives and sixty cars haul primarily farm products, but also paper products, chemical products, and oil. The line connects with CP and CN in Transcona.

The Saskatchewan Initiative

More than any other province, Saskatchewan has encouraged short lines. In 1989 the government enacted legislation approving the granting of loans to locally initiated efforts to acquire branch lines the CN and CP were proposing for abandonment. An earlier example might be considered the Southern Railway Corporation — a farmer-driven short line between Moose Jaw and Rockglen in southern Saskatchewan that hauled primarily grain. By 2010 nearly a dozen similar short lines were rumbling across the prairie landscape.

One of the first short lines under the new legislation was the Carlton Trail Railway. Based in Prince Albert, it took over operations for 140 kilometres of track between Saskatoon and Prince Albert from the CNR. Its facilities are in Prince Albert, where it owns one of the only two operating roundhouses in Canada. The line is operated by Omnitrax, a short line operator based in Denver.

Thunder Rail began its operations in 2005, between Arborfield and Carrot River on the CN line. At only 19.5 kilometres, it was considered too short to interest such short line operators as Omnitrax, leaving operations to Thunder Rail's staff of three. Six local individuals are qualified to operate the single locomotive.

Headquartered in Leader, Saskatchewan, the Great Sand Hills Railway controls 187 kilometres of track between Birstall, Alberta, and Swift Current, Saskatchewan. The company was chartered in 2008 and just a year later was running one-hundred-car trains.

The Torch River Railway between Choiceland and Nippawin met some initial resistance from the CPR, but once the proponents had a high profile private sector partner involved, the rail company agreed to sell the line. Soon, The Torch River Railway would be running five hundred cars a year.

Another of the major short line rail operators is the Great Western Railway (no relation to the long-defunct rail company of the same name that was based in Ontario and amalgamated with the Grand Trunk Railway in 1882).

A number of the short lines are operated by the Great Western Railway, which has forty sidings. Among the lines it operates are the Red Coat Road and Rail and the Fife Lake Railway. All together, it operates on 438 kilometres of what would otherwise have been ghost rail lines. It is headquartered in Shaunavon, Saskatchewan, and links with the CPR at Assiniboia and Swift Current. The Red Coat Road and Rail company runs between Pangman and Assiniboia, and it will be the first of the short lines to host a tour train operation.

Based in Ogema, the Southern Prairie Railway, with its ex-CPR coach and diesel engine, plans to run trains from its newly relocated CPR station.

The Rail Trails

Few of the Prairies' many abandoned rail lines have become rail trails, as has happened in Ontario and Quebec. The Rossburn Subdivision Trail in western Manitoba, and the Iron Horse Trail in Alberta, however, now form two of the longer such trails. Shorter rail trails may be found in Red Deer, Alberta; Naicam, Saskatchewan; and in Hamiota and Grosse Isle in Manitoba.

THE ROSSBURN SUBDIVISION TRAIL, RUSSELL TO NEEPAWA

This 170-kilometre-trail ventures from Neepawa in the east to Russell in the west. The trail is generally suitable for hikers, equestrians, and skiers, while also attracting its share of ATVs. It starts with some history at the Beautiful Plains Museum, situated in the 1902 Canadian Northern Railway divisional station in Neepawa, for it was here that the railway located its main line yards and offices for the next 160 kilometres of railway operation. From a point north of the station called Rossburn Junction, the CNo extended a branch line west, reaching Rossburn in 1905 and Russell in 1908.

The trail offers a cross-section of Manitoba's railway and natural heritage. In its eastern stretches, it crosses wide prairie landscapes, while the central portion follows small river valleys and the scenic shores of lakes such as Sandy Lake and Lake Beaufort, where cormorants and great blue herons abound. It passes through active and vibrant towns such as Sandy Lake and Russell, and others that have nearly died away, like Menzie, Silverton, and Vista. Birdtail is described as being a ghost town. Small wooden trestles lie en route near Vista and Elphinstone, while others have attracted the usual arsonists.

Several communities through which the trail passes have retained their grain elevators. In fact, the western trailhead at Russell lies by the town's lone grain elevator. Other grain elevators survive at Angusville, Oakburn, and Silverton. Scenic vistas occur at the intersection with the Desjarlais Trail, known as the Windy Viewpoint, while another awaits between Angusville and Rossburn.

Sandy Lake, about the halfway point, is a busy tourist town, where the CNo's class-3 station now serves as the office for a nearby campground. The former station grounds here serve as a trail head for trail users. A one-time station, now nearly hidden by a hedge at the north end of the hamlet of Vista, is in fact the CNo class-3 station from Rossburn. Rossburn, which itself served as the divisional point for this subdivision, offers historical interpretative plaques on the grounds where the station once stood. An elevator survives here as well.

THE IRON HORSE TRAIL, WASKATENAU, ALBERTA, TO HEINSBURG AND COLD LAKE

This hiking, skiing, and ATV trail follows the former CNR line between Waskatenau in the west and the ghost town of Heinsburg in the east, with a branch to Cold Lake. The rail line was part of a failed effort by the Canadian Northern Railway to access the settlements between Edmonton and North Battleford north of the North Saskatchewan River. Even after the CNR took over construction, the link was never completed. Eventually, the section east of Waskatenau was abandoned and has given the Prairies' one of its longest rail trails.

That portion from Waskatenau to Abilene Junction stretches for ninety-two kilometres and begins at a 1919 wooden trestle at the east end of the community. This high wooden trestle was originally twice today's length, but the ends were filled with earth.

The official trail head, however, lies in Smoky Lake by a well-preserved CNo class-3 rural-style station (as well as giant pumpkins). The trail leads east to Bellis, beyond which it crosses a trestle that is more than two hundred metres long. The next "station stop" of Vilna offers a main street that has been restored to resemble its more prosperous period and contains Alberta's oldest pool room, now a designated provincial heritage structure. Built in 1921 by Steve Pawluk, it operated as both a pool room and barber shop until 1996, after which it was acquired by a local heritage group.

Farther to the east, Saint Paul was established as a divisional point with the standard CNo class-3 station,

Rossburn, Manitoba, offers information plaques on the Rossburn Rail Trail.

lengthened to accommodate the needed facilities. Sadly, the grain elevators and the CNo station that stood through the 1980s are gone now, leaving little more than a barren field.

From Abilene Junction, the trail splits, with the northeast path leading ninety kilometres to Cold Lake. On this portion, before entering the picturesque lakeside town of Bonnyville, the trail features a winter warming hut modelled after a railway station and a one-time watering site for the steam locomotives. Another major trestle five hundred metres long crosses the Beaver River, and the trail finishes this leg in Cold Lake. The southeast branch leads to Elk Point and finally Heinsburg.

Odd names abound along the rail lines in the prairies, and Owlseye's origins remain obscure. Yet it was at one time a thriving railway town with stores, a station, and grain elevators. While only a few dwellings now mark the site, the yard of one such dwelling contains the village's portable style station.

The community of Elk Point has replicated their 1927 CN-style two-storey station beside the rail trail and uses it as an eco-information centre as well as for tourist information. The rail trail ends up in the ghost town of Heinsburg, where the water tower and station are preserved, and where the main street offers a row of weathered abandoned stores.

NAICAM RAIL TRAIL

This relatively short walking trail, just two kilometres long, follows the former CP line from the town of Naicam and heads from 3rd Street north into the open spaces around the town. The town has also retained its station, now a restaurant, as well as a pair of elevators.

EDMONTON

Edmonton enjoys a system of riverside trails. One of them, the Mill Creek ravine trail, follows the road bed of the Edmonton, Yukon and Pacific Railway (EY&P), a line whose sole purpose was to bridge the South Saskatchewan River and connect Edmonton with the CPR's then head of steel in Strathcona. A historic wooden trestle erected by the EY&P forms part of the trail.

HAMIOTA

The Pitlochery and Chumah trails both follow abandoned portions of the Canadian Pacific Railway, which built its tracks through Hamiota. While the Pitlochery leads hikers into a marshland habitat, the Chumah trail, which is also groomed for cross country skiing, takes the visitor into a more prairie-like grassland setting.

THE PRIME MERIDIAN TRAIL

This Manitoba rail trail follows the abandoned CN Inwood subdivision from Grosse Isle to Argyle, a distance of ten kilometres. It takes hikers, cyclists, and cross country skiers through grassland and farm fields. The Grosse Isle starting point coincides with a popular stop on the Prairie Dog Central Railway steam and diesel railway excursions.

Chapter Ten

Celebrating the Heritage

The Canadian Prairies celebrate their railway heritage in many ways. One of the most fitting ways to illustrate how the heritage of those rail lines affected the development of the land is in the many railway museums. Here have been gathered steam engines, stations, railway equipment, and, in a few cases, grain elevators and water towers.

Alberta

ALBERTA CENTRAL RAILWAY MUSEUM

Located a few kilometres southeast of Wetaskawin, Alberta, this growing collection of railway rolling stock is yet another example of the efforts being made all across the prairie provinces to celebrate the railway heritage that made them. The name comes from an actual railway line, the Alberta Central, which operated from 1913 until 1981, from Red Deer to Rocky Mountain House.

The main building is a slightly scaled down version of the Wetaskawin station (which still stands as well), and it depicts how railway operations took place in such a station. Visitors are pulled along a 1.5-kilometre-section of track by the only preserved example of an RS 32 diesel locomotive, which was built by the Montreal Locomotive Works. The heritage coach is a CPR buffet sleeper built in 1926 and named the *Mount Avalanche*.

Not to neglect that other prairie icon, in 2002 the museum added to its collection one of Alberta's oldest surviving grain elevators, built by the Alberta Grain Company in 1906 in Hobbema.

The recently acquired CPR RDC (Rail Diesel Electric) chrome dayliner (the cab is located in the front of the coach) served on Montreal's commuter lines from 1956 until 1977, and then as a VIA Rail coach until 1985, when the CPR used it as an instructional car. A little portable station from Hobbema represents the standard portable style of station that was built by the dozens and then shipped out to whatever community needed an instant station. This structure was built in 1902 and removed in the 1920s, when the CPR replaced it with a larger structure.

ALBERTA RAILWAY MUSEUM

In 1968 the Alberta Pioneer Railway Association was formed in the Cromdale streetcar barns of Edmonton. But the facility was too small, and in 1976 the group moved their historic collection to a rural location north of Edmonton on the former Canadian Northern Railway's Coronado subdivision. Since that time, the dedicated group has assembled an impressive collection of railway equipment.

The stars of the museum are two "F" series streamline diesel locomotives formerly operated by VIA Rail. In 1999 a rare refrigerator car came to the museum from the Alberta Prairie Railway excursion in Stettler. Another rare find is what is called a "Box Baggage" car, in other words, a box car refitted to function as a baggage and mail car. It is painted in the CN green-and-gold scheme. Also painted in the green and gold is an express baggage and mail car, built in 1937 and handed to the Alberta Railway Museum (ARM) in 1995. Such cars were equipped with catch bars that would grab the mail sack from the catch on the station platform. Inside the mail car, clerks would sort the mail into mail sacks for specific stations and simply toss them out as they passed the station.

A 1939 express baggage car came to the museum in 1994 from the Canadian forces base. It is typical of baggage cars that raced across the country on the famous silk trains. To get the silk from the west coast to New York, these silk trains, which could consist of two dozen such cars, had right of way over all other trains.

The museum has arranged its equipment into train sets, which include a "CNR passenger train," headed by a pair of 1957 diesel locomotives; a "Northern Alberta Railway work train"; a prairie "mixed train," headed by a 1913 CNo steam locomotive, number 1392; and a "Northern Alberta Railway passenger train," headed by a 1927 steam locomotive used originally by the Edmonton, Dunvegan and BC Railway (which later became the NAR).

Among the ARM's buildings are the St. Albert CNo station, which was built in 1909 northwest of Edmonton. The station serves as the museum's gift shop and ticket office. A much trickier operation was moving the bulky water tower from Gibbons. A glimpse inside gives the visitor a rare look at how these now-vanished structures provided the vital water to the steam locomotives.

ARDROSSAN: KATIE'S CROSSING

Located near the railway trestle at Ardrossan, there is a remarkable collection of railway rolling stock that forms Katie's Crossing Restaurant and Café. The collection includes two Pullman coaches, two cabooses, and a boxcar that can be used as a stage. Ardrossan is about twenty kilometres southeast of Edmonton.

ASPEN CROSSING

Located southeast of Calgary, this multi-faceted commercial operation is part garden centre, part campground, and part dining experience — all focusing on the area's railway heritage. The most visible and striking component is the maroon-coloured business car. Built by the CPR in 1887, it originally carried CPR executives and other business types across the country in luxury. As recently as 1962, photos show John Diefenbaker campaigning from the rear platform of the coach. Following its career as a rail car, it ended up in Edmonton as part of the Sidetrack Café. In 2006 the owners of Aspen Crossing mounted it on a flatbed truck and moved it to the Aspen Crossing grounds. Here, it serves as a restaurant and occasionally hosts dinner theatre as well. A replica station serves as a garden centre, while the actual portable-type station from neighbouring Mossleigh rests nearby. In the campground area, more railway heritage presents itself in the form of a pair of cabooses, which have been converted into accommodations.

BEISEKER RAILWAY MUSEUM

Located on a section of the Trans Canada Trail, this recent museum occupies an abandoned portion of the CPR's Langdon subdivision line. Equipment includes diesels numbered *8017*, built by the CPR in 1959; and *8704*, built by the CN in 1958; as well as six various boxcars. The site lies two blocks south of Beiseker's municipal office, which is situated in the former CPR station. The property is owned by Alberta Trailnet, a partner with the Trans Canada Trail.

CALGARY'S HERITAGE PARK

The Prairies' most extensive homage to its railway heritage lies within the heritage park at Calgary. While this is a park designed to depict the many stages of Calgary's growth, from aboriginal times up to the 1930s, it includes the heritage of the Prairies' railway era. It does so by recreating a typical prairie railway town with a variety of heritage buildings, including four original CPR stations. The station from Midnapore is a CPR A-2 WLS: two storeys with a dormer on the second storey roof. It was built in 1910 by the CPR in the nearby community of Midnapore and given to the heritage park in 1964 for $1. It now serves as the headquarters for the park's historical operations.

The Shepard station, a similar style save for the shape of the dormer, was moved to the park in 1970 and stands at the head of the Boomtown main street. It is here that visitors can board a genuine steam train drawn by a 1944 steam engine, either number *2023* or *2024*, and ride in some of Canada's oldest surviving passenger coaches. Other stations along the park's track include the CPR's Laggan station, a small log station that remained in use until 1909, when the current Lake Louise station, also log, was built to serve the growing numbers of tourists flocking to the Chateau Lake Louise. The old Laggan station remained as a storage facility until 1976, when it was moved to the park. The Bowell CPR station built in 1909 is an example of a portable station that would be prefabricated and then transported to whatever community quickly needed a small station building.

Aspen Crossing provides fine dining in a converted coach.

The car shop and roundhouse are replicas to depict the scene at a typical divisional point along the railway. A replica of a square water tower was built here as well, to illustrate this forgotten feature of Canada's rail lines, although the more common style of water tower was the eight-sided variety. The park's tower was built in 1973 to provide water for the two operating steam engines. The park also has an impressive roster of railway equipment, including the 1905 steam engine *2018*, one of five steam engines in the collection, as well as seven coaches, three of which date to the 1880s. Cabooses, tank cars, flat cars, and a mail car are also among the collection, most of which is stored in the car shop.

The Park's most recent addition is a historic CPR coach, the *River Forth*. Built as an observation car at Montreal's Angus shops in 1929, it saw service on the CPR's popular transcontinental runs. In 1944 it became the *Cape Knox* and was converted to a sleeper car, and then in 1964 was again changed, this time to a business car. It served out its final days in Winnipeg as a work car and was subsequently stored in Calgary's Ogden Yards.

CHAMPION PARK, ALDERSYDE

For drivers travelling on Highway 2 between Calgary and Lethbridge, there is a railway "park" that virtually appears out of nowhere, for there are no signs that announce it, nor is it near any rail line past or present. The reason is that the collection of buildings and rolling stock is private. The collection was amassed by the Knowlton family in honour of Ted Knowlton, who worked as a CPR station master for forty-eight years. The focus is on the CPR's Champion station, which was relocated to the family property. The rolling stock features a CPR camel-back diesel (number 12), a box car, a tank car, two cabooses, and the pride of the fleet, the CPR executive car, *Saskatchewan*, which was

built in 1929 and transported to this location in 1983, where it has been restored. So impressive is this tribute to the heritage of the CPR that the railway's then-president Norris "Buck" Crump presided at Champion Park's "last spike" ceremony to honour the 100th anniversary of his railway. Although the collection is clearly visible from the road, access is by invitation only.

FORT EDMONTON PARK

This park was created in 1969 to depict the evolution of the city of Edmonton, starting with the 1846 fort and continuing to streets that depict 1885, 1905, and 1920. While there are no heritage stations or other historic railway structures, the equipment is genuine enough. Visitors can board a steam train hauled by a 1919 Baldwin steam locomotive, number 17. Built in Philadelphia in 1919, it served a long life hauling logs in Oakdale, Louisiana, until 1969, when it was retired. It was brought to the park in 1977 and now carries tourists in three "Canadian Northern" coaches around the park's perimeter from its purpose-built station. The Edmonton Radial Railway Society offers rides on its vintage streetcars and maintains its shops here. The shops house nearly twenty tram cars, some of which pre-date the First World War. There is also a 1912 electric locomotive.

MCLENNAN: THE GOLDEN COACH NORTHERN ALBERTA RAILWAY MUSEUM

The rails that struck out northwesterly from Edmonton to reach Peace Country are often given scant attention in the history of Canada's rail lore, especially when compared to the focus in song, literature, and film on the CPR, Canada's "National Dream." If anything, the rails to Peace Country were more a regional dream. Located in McLennan, Alberta, the "golden coach" is a relic from passenger days on the Northern Alberta Railway. In 1914 the town of McLennan became a divisional point for the railway and a substantial station was built, and in later years that building was replaced with a more modern structure. Along with presenting a caboose, the "Golden Coach Museum" recounts the story of the rails to Peace Country, helping to bring to life an otherwise underappreciated chapter in the railway heritage of the prairies. The coach itself was a NAR sleeping car known as the *Sexsmith*.

TOFIELD: THE FOOTLOOSE CABOOSE LODGE

Like Aspen Crossing, the Footloose Caboose Lodge is also a railway-themed private operation. Dining is available in the 1909 CPR observation car, the *Mount Lefroy*, while guests can sleep in one of two steel railway cabooses, built by the CNR and BC Rail respectively. There are seven cabooses on the property. The operation begin in 1995 when the first caboose arrived. The *Mount Lefroy* offered cross-country passenger service until 1942, when it was sold to Northern Alberta Railway. It then languished untended until 1991, when it was acquired by the current owners. The site also features the GTP's Duffield station, one of that line's rural type stations. It remained in private hands from its closing in 1962 until its move to the present site, where it now serves as the owners' residence. This interesting heritage operation lies near Tofield, about sixty kilometres southeast of Edmonton.

WAINWRIGHT RAIL PARK

This park is a work of love by the volunteers of the Wainwright Railway Preservation Society and its president Don McGuire. The park opened in 1995 and its collection today includes a pair of CN diesel engines, a VIA Rail generating van, speeders, and the CN sleeper coach the *Matapedia*, which was built in 1923 and is now

painted in the later CN green-and-gold paint scheme. The park's wooden caboose was converted by the CNR in 1943 from an original Grand Trunk boxcar that had been built in 1912. The most recent addition was a canola tank car from Nipawin. Other equipment on display includes box cars and a flat car, as well as two ploughs and a spreader. One of the ploughs built for single tracks has a double scoop, while that built for double tracks has a single side scoop.

Saskatchewan

MELVILLE REGIONAL PARK

Melville is doubly enriched by having not only one of the province's most impressive heritage stations but also a well-stocked railway museum. The museum display is focused around the GTP station from the village of Duff, and it covers the line's two hundred country stations found along both the GTP and NTR, from Quebec to the Pacific. The building is one and a half storeys, with a small octagonal dormer above the operator's bay window. Displayed equipment includes a CNR caboose manufactured in Winnipeg in 1957, a flat car, a 1918 box car, and a vintage steam locomotive. Numbered *5114*, this CN Pacific-class steam engine displays a 4-6-2 wheel configuration and was manufactured in the Montreal Locomotive Works in 1918. The display recreates a steam engine and train stopped in front of a typical prairie station. To add further to the authenticity, the equipment itself was all used along the GTP line through Melville.

THE SASKATCHEWAN RAILWAY MUSEUM, SASKATOON

This impressive collection of buildings and rolling stock is located on Highway 60 a short distance west of Saskatoon on what was originally the CNo's Eaton Siding. From 1914–1920, the siding was the site of one of Canada's infamous internment camps during the war. Most of those detained at the Eaton Siding camp were of Ukrainian origin. After the war, the CNR renamed it the Hawker Siding.

In 1990 the Saskatchewan Railway Museum moved its collection onto the site, which has since grown steadily. It now includes, among the rolling stock, three diesel switch engines, which are traditionally much smaller than the main line engines, as well as a pair of smaller diesels formerly operated by Saskatchewan Power. The 1913 Pullman sleeper known as the *Kirkella* continued a roll on a work train until 1996. In addition the museum includes four box cars, four cabooses, three flat cars, three streetcars, and a tanker. Buildings include a Canadian Northern bunkhouse from Maymont and a portable station from Brisbin.

One of the more unusual structures, one that ranks as scarcer than stations and water towers, is a switching tower formerly located at Oban between Biggar and Battleford. It was built by the GTP to protect its crossing with the CPR track at that location. Inside the structure, levers controlled the eight sets of semaphores, four of which were located at the immediate crossing, and four about half a kilometre farther out to warn the train engineers in advance. The tower was moved to the museum in 1990.

WESTERN DEVELOPMENT MUSEUMS, MOOSE JAW AND NORTH BATTLEFORD

In addition to its interior exhibits, the Moose Jaw Western Development Museum (WDM) once again operates a steam driven short line. Admittedly, the line is confined to the grounds of the museum, but it is Saskatchewan's only steam train operation. The engine is a refurbished Vulcan steam locomotive built in 1914 by the Vulcan Iron Works in Wilkes-Barre, Pennsylvania.

A railway exhibit inside the vast building includes a mock-up of a prairie station, as well as a CPR steam locomotive, *2634*, which was built in 1913, and a CPR combination passenger and baggage coach. The indoor display also includes a CPR wooden caboose and a 1934 Buick track inspection car.

In contrast to the WDM in Moose Jaw, the one in North Battleford is primarily an outdoor display of a prairie town as it may have appeared in the days of rail. Here, a Canadian Northern steam engine, *1158*, a ten-wheeler built in Montreal in 1913, heads a "prairie train," which includes a CN stock car, flat car, box car, and caboose. The rolling stock stands on a track beside what was the St. Albert, Alberta, class-4 CNo train station. Rounding out the railway heritage landscape is a grain elevator that formerly stood in Keatley and was moved to the museum in 1983.

Saskatchewan has, in fact, four different WDM locations, all of which tell their own compelling stories of prairie development. Yorkton's features the "Story of People," while Saskatoon's focuses on a "1910 Boomtown" (and has 1905 steam engine on display).

Manitoba

FORT LA REINE MUSEUM, PORTAGE LA PRAIRIE

While the Fort la Reine Museum focuses largely on the wide range of early homes on the prairies, it contains one of the more interesting rail cars found anywhere on the prairies, if not the rarest. And that is the actual railcar that William Van Horne used when constructing the Canadian Pacific Railway west of Winnipeg in the early

1880s. Beside it is *Car #21*, a superintendent's car. With such cars, the business of operating the railway could take place while actually travelling the line. This is one of only two surviving superintendents' cars of the twenty-two that were built. The museum is about two kilometres east of the town's two stations and is within view of the rail lines. It is located at the intersection of Saskatchewan Avenue and the Highway 1 bypass.

WINNIPEG

The Forks

With rail lines converging on the relatively narrow strip of land between Lake Winnipeg and the U.S. border, the forks of the Red and Assiniboine Rivers became a major hub for several rail lines. Among the earliest to arrive at the forks was the Northern Pacific and Manitoba Railway (NP&M), which arrived in 1886 and built its repair shops

Some of the historic railway cars in the Alberta Central Railway Museum near Wetaskiwin, Alberta.

at the forks in 1889. Engines would enter through large gates and halt atop a pit, from which repairs would be undertaken. Soon after came the Canadian Northern and Grand Trunk Pacific Railways. Although rivals, they collaborated to build Winnipeg's massive Union Station. But the site of the forks also became the site of major rail yards along with a stable and a cartage building. The buildings and bridges headquarters moved into the NP&M repair shop. The CPR had chosen a route to the north of the forks and was not part of the convergence here.

With the abandonment of the yards by the CNR, demolition seemed a temptation. Instead, a consortium known as the North Forks Portage Partnership has converted the many historic structures into one of Winnipeg's leading tourist attractions, which is known simply as the Forks. While the CNo and NP&M stables were joined to become the Forks market, the cartage building, known as the Johnson Terminal, is now a market building. But the most historic structure of all, the NP&M repair shop, now houses the Winnipeg Children's Museum. Sadly, however, an unsympathetic addition has obscured much of the exterior. The Children's Museum displays a 1910 Pullman combination coach and replica Winnipeg streetcar. On the grounds of the Forks, near the market, are a 1926 CPR parlour car and a 1924 combination passenger coach.

Winnipeg Railway Museum

This magnificent collection of railway rolling stock is situated appropriately in one the most significant and elegant railway buildings in the Prairies: Winnipeg's Union Station. And here one finds one of Canada's most significant steam locomotives, the *Countess of Dufferin*. It was the first steam engine to arrive on the prairies, having been carried by the steamer *Selkirk* down the Red River from Fisher's Landing in Minnesota, after which it had been carried by the Saint

Paul and Pacific Railroad. Renumbered from CPR 2 to CPR 1, it was named after the wife of Canada's governor general at the time, Viscount Lord Dufferin. Accompanied by a caboose, tender, and six flat cars, it docked in the early morning of October 8, 1877. It ran for twenty years as a wood-burner before being replaced by the more efficient coal-fired steam locomotives. After struggling on for a few more years hauling lumber, the historic engine was left in pieces in the lumberyard. In 1909 it was rediscovered and donated to the City of Winnipeg, which reconditioned it and put it on display near the CPR station. In 1994 it came to the Winnipeg Railway Museum, where it rests on track number 1.

Also on display is another locomotive first, the CN GMD1, built in 1959 and the first of its series. The museum also displays nearly twenty pieces of railway equipment, including three baggage cars, a boxcar, and a caboose. Beyond a wall, VIA Rail rumbles in and out, carrying passengers on its historic transcontinental *Canadian*, or on the popular Churchill train.

Other sites in and around Winnipeg also display the community's steam heritage. Steam engine *2747*, the first to be built in the Transcona shops by the CNR, stands on Plessis Road in Transcona. Number *6043*, the last steam engine to run on CNR line, finally running out of steam in 1964, stands in Winnipeg's Assiniboine Park.

Back to the Future: Heritage Rail Excursions

In addition to the remarkable assembly of railway museums throughout the Prairies, there are a few tour trains that venture along historic rails, offering their riders a living glimpse into the Prairies' rail heritage.

STETTLER, ALBERTA: PRAIRIE STEAM TOURS

Although Canadian railways ceased using steam locomotives in the 1960s, a large gleaming black steam engine still puffs across the countryside between Stettler and Meeting Creek, Alberta. This is the famous *6060*. It was built in Montreal in 1944 to help deal with the increase in passenger and freight traffic during the Second World War. In order to rush it into service, the configuration was made more efficient. A one-piece metal frame, more refined water distribution system, and more efficient heating system meant it was quicker and less costly to build. Following the war, *6060* began its role in transcontinental passenger service. Its wheel arrangement (known as a 4-8-4) made it ideal for travel through the steep and twisting mountain grades. Then, following a brief stint of using it as a tour train in Ontario, in 1980 the CNR donated the steam engine to Alberta to celebrate that province's 75th anniversary. The steam engine was promptly dubbed "The Spirit of Alberta" by the Rocky Mountain Rail Society. Of the twenty steam engines built by CN in this style, that used at Stettler is the only engine to remain in service. Two others survive but are on static display only.

The tour train began operation in 1990 from a new specially built station in Stettler on the site of the original CNo divisional station (now located in Stettler's Town and Country Park). In addition to *6060*, the train may also be pulled by a smaller sixty-two-foot 1920 Baldwin-class engine, also from the CNR. The third engine is a former CN SW1200 diesel built in 1957. The engines haul a set of coaches, some of which date back to 1919.

These excursions take travellers across country to the original CNo divisional station at Big Valley. Here, the travellers disembark to tour either the museum in the station or the roundhouse ruins. A grain elevator and coach remain on-site as well. En route, the train passes the Fenn Big Valley oil fields and the Fenn general store. Dinner trains, theatre trains, and school excursions are among the more popular itineraries. Excursions last about two hours each way.

Because of the enormous popularity of the APR excursions, especially those under steam, work began in 2011 to extend the line northward to eventually reach Donalda, twenty-five kilometres away. In 2009 the Government of Canada allocated $3.2 million through the Community Adjustment Fund to help with the project. The extension is being spearheaded by the East Central Alberta Heritage Society.

INKSTER, MANITOBA: THE PRAIRIE DOG CENTRAL RAILWAY

Operated by the Vintage Locomotive Society of Winnipeg, the Prairie Dog Central Railway (PDC) has been puffing across the Manitoba countryside since 1970. Its original route, which it followed for four years, was along Wilkes Boulevard on the Canadian National Railway's Cabot subdivision. In 1975 it switched to the Oak Point Subdivision, which it used for the next twenty years. The rail line had been built by the Canadian Northern Railway between 1905 and 1910 and was part of that ambitious little line's Trans-Canada route, which became the CNR.

Then, typically, the CNR not only advised that it was abandoning that subdivision but was also evicting the organization from the CN's Transcona facilities, where they had been storing their equipment. Faced with its potential demise, the PDC began fundraising to build new facilities and to relocate its historic station, the federally designated St. James station. The PDC then purchased the Oak Point subdivision and now recreates Manitoba's railway heritage with no fear of the CNR.

The route takes passengers on vintage coaches pulled alternately by steam and diesel. The route leads north-westerly through Grosse Point, where a small waiting shelter functions as the station. A grain elevator remains at Warren and offers train goers a glimpse of how grain elevators once functioned. And, oh yes, the train might encounter some "train robbers" en route.

The steam engine itself was built in 1882 by the CPR at a cost of $12,500 and is the oldest operating steam engine in Canada. In fact, it was used in the TV adaptation of Pierre Berton's book, *The National Dream*, which tells the story of the building of the CPR. The PDC also uses a pair of diesel locomotives, *4138* having been donated by the Grand Trunk Western Railroad and Diesel *1685* by the Burlington Santa Fe Northern in 2010. The five vintage coaches date between 1906 and 1913, all having been built for Great Winnipeg Water District Railway.

The Prairie Dog Central was one of the first of the prairie tour trains to use steam.

CPR *2816*, CALGARY

Known also as the *Empress*, steam engine number *2816* was built in Montreal in 1929 and operated on high-speed trains between Winnipeg and Calgary. With its larger fire box and higher steam pressure, it was able to exceed seventy miles per hour. Known also as a Hudson-class steam locomotive, it is the only survivor of the twenty originally built between 1929 and 1930. It served out its final years hauling commuter trains between Montreal and Rigaud before being retired in 1960. After being on static display for a number of years, the CPR reacquired the monster in 1998, restoring it to operating condition, only this time using oil rather than coal. Based in Calgary, it operates along the CPR lines on an irregular schedule as a roving ambassador for the railway.

THE ROYAL CANADIAN PACIFIC, CPR CALGARY

This magnificent train recalls the days of luxury rail travel. The business cars are housed in the Canadian Pacific Pavilion of Calgary's Palliser Hotel and were built in a specialized shop in Montreal created in 1902 by CPR president William C. Van Horne. Each, of course, has its own distinctive name. The *Strathcona*, *Van Horne*, and *Royal Wentworth* were built in 1926 and 1927 and feature state rooms, a vestibule, and a dining area. The *Banffshire* and the *N.R. Crump* were built as sleepers and offer travellers comfortable accommodations on the rail tours. The 1931 sleeper known as the *Craigallechie* now serves as a dining car. But the highlight of the fleet is the *Mount Stephen*, built as the president's day car, and it features the rear porch from which many a dignitary has proffered a royal wave or two.

EDMONTON RADIAL RAILWAY SOCIETY

The Edmonton Radial Railway Society (ERRS) has been instrumental in celebrating a distinctive part of Canada's rail heritage. A volunteer organization, as so many are, the ERRS began in 1980, determined to restore a streetcar — Edmonton Streetcar #1. From that beginning, the group has worked to restore eight streetcars to operational condition, in addition to three that have been restored but do not operate. In the thirty years after streetcar service began, Edmonton, like so many other short-sighted Canadian cities, pulled their streetcars off the tracks. Most were sold for scrap or to other systems outside of Canada.

The ERRS collection can now boast of four Edmonton units, two from the Toronto area, one from each Saskatoon and Regina, and three from such distant places as Hannover, Germany; Melbourne, Australia; and Osaka, Japan. When in 1995 the CPR ended its rail traffic across Edmonton's famous High Level bridge, the ERRS set to work re-installing overhead wires.

Finally, in 2011 an original Edmonton streetcar, #33, restored to its 1912 condition, made its debut run, thus restoring a display of original rail heritage to the city of Edmonton.

SOUTHERN PRAIRIE RAILWAY, OGEMA

After thirty-three years of storing grain, the Ogema Heritage Railway Association lugged the large CPR station, originally built at Simpson, back to its rightful place at the foot of Ogema's historic main street, where the town's original and identical station had once stood. The organization then set about to acquire railway equipment with which to operate a tour train. To start, they obtained a GE forty-four-ton diesel engine from the Maine Central Railway. Then it was the vintage CPR baggage express car *4747* — built in 1952 by Canadian Car and foundry in Montreal, it served out its days as service equipment in Moose Jaw. But the most elegant of the rolling stock is the seventy-seat 1920 Pullman coach built for the Delaware, Lackawanna and Western Railroad. The trains will travel the Red Coat Road and Rail short line between Ogema and Assiniboia.

VIA RAIL: THE LIVING LEGACY

There is no better way to experience the railway heritage of the prairies than to cross them on the last of the scheduled passenger trains, those of VIA Rail. VIA Rail Canada was formed in 1978 to take over the passenger services of the CN and CP. More interested in hauling freight than people, the two companies had been accused of deliberately making passenger travel as inconvenient as

VIA Rail's popular cross-country train, the legendary Canadian, *pauses at Portage la Prairie, Manitoba*

possible so that passengers would abandon the trains and allow the railways to justify abandoning the service. But the demand wouldn't go away, and in a typical Canadian compromise, VIA Rail was formed. But even then, politicians ignored the travelling needs of Canadians, and transportation ministers like Jean Luc Pepin and Benoit Bouchard set about dismantling much of Canada's rail passenger service. In the case of Pepin, the subsequent government of Brian Mulroney restored most of those cuts, only to inflict more damaging cuts of its own in 1990, when, despite outrage from Canadians, Bouchard eliminated half of VIA's trains.

Happier times returned when a new Liberal transport minister, David Collenette, announced a VIA renaissance, with new equipment and new stations, but regrettably no restoration of the discontinued runs.

Still, there is no experience as genuine as seeing the prairies from the seat of a train. While VIA's schedule between Edmonton and Saskatoon occurs during the night, that between Saskatoon and Winnipeg occurs during the daylight in both directions. A midday departure from Winnipeg brings riders to Saskatoon in late evening, while a morning departure from Saskatoon brings the train to Winnipeg around the dinner hour. En route, the train may stop at waiting shelters beside the historic GTP stations at Melville and Rivers.

The best feature of all is that the excursions occur on Canada's most elegant and historic train, and one of the ten most beautiful trains in the world, the *Canadian*. The train set was brought into service by the CPR in the mid 1950s to try and revitalize passenger service on their line. Its chrome coaches feature the popular dome cars and the iconic "bullet lounge" at the rear, while sleeping cars provide a comfortable rest for the multi-day trip.

Another of VIA's more popular multi-day excursions is that which reaches into the subarctic tundra at Churchill, Manitoba. This two-night trip follows the tracks of the legendary Hudson Bay Railway. Many travellers on this train may stay over in the northern ocean port to embark on outings to view the region's polar bears. Others, however, are residents of the many First Nations communities that line the track and for whom the train is their only means of transport. En route, the train may stop at such historic stations as Portage la Prairie, Roblin, Dauphin, Canora, The Pas, and Gillam before arriving at the large steep-roofed station in Churchill. Travellers may notice the coaches of the Keewatin Railway while passing The Pas. These are run by the region's First Nations and make twice-weekly trips to Pukatawagan on the Lynn Lake branch line.

Those not travelling on the trains may find that the best location for train watching is in Portage la Prairie, Manitoba. Here, the historic main lines of both the CN and CP run within metres of each other, guarded by their respective heritage stations. Each Saturday, both the *Canadian* and the Churchill passenger trains pass the station within a few hours of each other, and may even stop, while freight trains rumble past at frequent intervals. Such is the living railway heritage of the Prairie Provinces.

Notes

1. Leonard F. Earl, "The Hudson Bay Railway," *The Manitoba Historical Society: MHS Transactions* 3, no. 14 (1957–58).

2. **Anti-black immigration policies**
   Attracted by such promotional literature as the "Last Best West," African Americans began to immigrate to Canada's Prairies during the 1880s. Their arrivals prompted protests from business communities in both Edmonton and Winnipeg. Although the federal government resisted the pressure to ban such immigration outright, they did impose such indirect techniques as refusing to send them literature on how to apply and subjected them to arbitrary medical examinations that deemed them to be physically unfit to settle in the harsh conditions of the area.

   Chinese Head Tax
   To help build its railway as cheaply as possible, the CPR brought fifteen thousand labourers from China, paying them only a fraction of what whites received. Alarmed at these numbers, British Columbia tried and failed to legislate against further immigration. In 1885 the federal government passed the Chinese Immigration Act, requiring Chinese immigrants pay $50 to enter the country, an amount which later rose to $500. Male immigrants were further forbidden from bringing their wives with them. The tax was finally abolished in 1923.

   Continuous Journey
   Bowing to western racism, in 1908 the federal government acted to discourage Indian immigration. Warned by the British government not to prohibit it outright, the new law rather stipulated that Indian immigrants had to travel by a continuous journey with no en route stops. Because ships that travelled that distance usually had to stop along the way, the restriction effectively halted such immigration. By the 1920s, a mere 1,300 people had immigrated to Canada from India. The law remained on the books until 1947.

   Source: The Canadian Encyclopedia.

3. Terry Patterson, "A Trip Through Time in Transcona," *Manitoba History* 15 (1987).

4. James H. Gray's seminal work on prairie prostitution, *Red Lights on the Prairies*, (Toronto: MacMillan, 1971), also highlights the red light sagas of places like Calgary, where the trade focused on 6th Avenue and 9th Avenue by the station, and Annabelle and MacFarlane Streets near Winnipeg's Point Douglas district. In Regina the red light trade seemed to concentrate around Ottawa and Tenth Avenue, near the station, although Moose Jaw was also considered to be Regina's red light district. A dozen brothels were located within a five minute walk of Saskatoon's CNo station.

5. The historical information on Empress is thanks to Pat Donaldson and the "That's Empressive" website.

6. Charles Bohi and Les Kozma have compiled a complete roster of railway stations in western Canada and catalogued them in accordance with their respective station styles, the subdivisions where they appeared, and the year in which they were built: *Canadian National's Western Stations*, (Markham: Fitzhenry & Whiteside, 2002); *Canadian Pacific's Western Depots*, (David City, Nebraska: South Platte Press, 1993).

7. Bruce Ballantine of the Bytown Railway Society carried out a census of Canada's railway stations, published in 1998 by the Bytown Railway Society as *The Guide to Canada's Railway Stations*. Station inventories can also be found on the Railway Station Historical Society website.

8. The Hotel MacDonald was good enough to make available a photocopy of the hotel's history.

9. Susan Rozniatowski, "Fallen Splendour: The Challener Murals of the Royal Alexandra Hotel," *Manitoba History*, no. 42 (2001–02).

10. Saskatchewan Heritage Foundation. *Saskatchewan Grain Elevators: An Inventory of Grain Handling Facilities.* Saskatoon, 2010.

11. Herrington R., *Saskatchewan Road and Railway Bridges to 1950*, Heritage Resources Branch, Saskatchewan Culture Youth and Recreation, March 31, 2007

12. David Malaher. "Port Nelson and the Hudson Bay Railway," *Manitoba History*, no. 8 (1984).

Bibliography

BOOKS

Ballentyne, Bruce. *Canadian Railway Station Guide.* Ottawa: The Bytown Railway Society, 1998.

Barris, Theodore. *Fire Canoe: Prairie Steamboat Days Revisited.* Toronto: McClelland & Stewart, 1977.

Bickle, Ian. *Turmoil and Triumph: The Controversial Railroad to Hudson Bay.* Calgary: Detselig Enterprises Ltd., 1995.

Bohi, Charles. *The Canadian National's Western Depots.* Toronto: Fitzhenry and Whiteisde, 1977.

Bohi, Charles and Les Kozma. *Canadian Pacific's Western Depots: The Country Stations in Western Canada.* David City, Nebraska: South Platte Press, 1993.

Butterfield, Daid K. *If Walls Could Talk: Manitoba's Best Buildings Explained and Explored.* Winnipeg: Great Plains Publishing, 2000.

Friesen, Gerald. *The Canadian Prairies: A History.* Toronto: University of Toronto Press, 1987.

Gibbon, John Murray. *Steel of Empire: A Romantic History of the Canadian Pacific Railway.* Toronto: McClelland & Stewart, 1935.

Glazebrook, G.P. De T. *History of Transportation in Canada.* Toronto: McClelland & Stewart, 1964.

Gray, James H. *Red Lights on the Prairies.* Toronto: Macmillan, 1971.

Herrington, A. *Saskatchewan Road and Railway Bridges to 1950: Inventory.* Saskatchewan Culture, Youth and Recreation, Heritage Resources Branch: 2007.

MacKay, Donald. *The People's Railway: A History of Canadian National.* Vancouver: Douglas & McIntyre, 1972.

McKee, William. *Trail of Iron: The CPR and the Birth of the West, 1880–1930.* Vancouver: Douglas & McIntyre, 1983.

McLennan, David. *Our Towns: Saskatchewan Communities from Abbey to Zenon Park.* Regina: University of Regina, Canadian Plains Research Centre, 2008.

Mulligan, Helen and Wanda Ryder. *Ghost Towns of Manitoba.* Surrey: Heritage House Publishing Company Ltd., 1985.

Regehr, T.D. *The Canadian Northern Railway: The Pioneering Road of the Northern Prairies, 1895–1918.* Toronto: Macmillan of Canada, 1976.

Saskatchewan Heritage Foundation. *Saskatchewan Grain Elevators: An Inventory of Grain Handling Facilities.* Saskatoon, 2010.

Silversides, Brock. *Prairie Sentinel: The Story of the Canadian Grain Elevator.* Calgary: Fifth House, 1997.

Thompson, John H. *Forging the Canadian West.* Toronto: Oxford University Press, 1998.

Waiser, W.A. *Saskatchewan: A New History.* Calgary: Fifth House, 2006.

Warkentin, John. *The Western Interior of Canada: A Record of Geographic Discovery, 1612–1917.* Toronto: McClelland & Stewart, 1964.

Wetherell, Donald Grant. *Town Life: Main Street and the Evolution of Small Town Alberta, 1880–1947.* Edmonton: University of Alberta Press, 1995.

JOURNALS, MAGAZINES, AND DOCUMENTS

"An Alberta Rose by Any Other Name." *CP Rail System News* 26, no. 2 (1996).

"CP Rail in Alberta Today." *CP Rail System News* 26, no. 3 (1996).

Earl, Leonard F. "The Hudson Bay Railway." *Manitoba Historical Society Transactions* 3, no. 14 (1957–58).

Government of Saskatchewan. "Minister Opens Saskatchewan's 10th Shortline Railway." October 15, 2009.

Government of Saskatchewan. "Moose Jaw's River Street to be Redeveloped." August 8, 2000.

Grover, Sheila. "The Northern Pacific and Manitoba Railway Engine House." *Manitoba History*, no. 10 (1985).

Herzog, Lawrence. "A Grand and Glorious Station." *Edmonton Real Estate Weekly* 23, no. 2 (2005).

Herzog, Lawrence. "When the Rails Led to Edmonton" *Edmonton Real Estate Weekly* 23, no. 31 (2005).

Jones, Dave. "From Cow Town to Now Town." *CP Rail System News* 26, no. 2 (1996).

Malaher, David. "Port Nelson and the Hudson Bay Railway," *Manitoba History*, no. 8 (1984).

Patterson, Terry. "A Trip Through Time in Transcona," *Manitoba History*, no. 13 (1987).

Rozniatowksi, Susan Moffatt. "A Fallen Splendour: The Challener Murals of the Royal Alexandra Hotel." *The Manitoba History*, no. 42, (2001–02).

"Warner Elevator Row." *Alberta Register of Historic Places — Heritage Management Resources Information System.*

NEWSPAPERS

Bernhardt, Darren. "Biggar Rallies to Save Historic Rail Roundhouse." *Star Phoenix*, October 30, 2007.

"Biggar Roundhouse Put on Endangered List," *Star Phoenix*, May 2, 2008.

Catherwood, Kristin. "Radville Station Undergoes Transformation." *Radville and Deep South Star*, September 1, 2009.

Halliday, Dave. "Historic Grain Elevators an Indelible Link to Alberta's Pioneer Roots." *North Shore News.*

"Old-Fashioned Pizza Party Spices up Rowley." *Drumheller Mail*, August 21, 2009.

Pacholik, Barb. "Fire Destroys Historic Grain Elevator in Fleming." *Regina Leader-Post*, February 9, 2010.

Rance, Laura. "Short line railroads under threat." *Winnipeg Free Press*, September 9, 2011.

Siamandas, George. "Winnipeg's Historic Bridges." *The Winnipeg Time Machine, Feb 5, 2007.*

WEBSITES

All links were accurate as of March 29, 2012.

Cranberry Heritage Museum. "Acquisition of Cranberry Portage Railway Station." *http://cpmuseum.ca.*

"Alberta Central Railway Museum." *www.abcentralrailway. com.*

"Alberta Prairie Railway Excursions." *www.absteamtrain. com.*

"Alberta's Iron Horse Trail," *www.ironhorsetrail.ca/index. html.*

Atlas of Alberta Railways. *http://railways.library.ualberta. ca/.*

Bachusky, Johnnie, "Rowley Alberta: The Never Say Die Prairie Town." Alberta Online Encyclopedia, Heritage Community Foundation. *www.abheritage. ca/albertans/bachusky/rowley_1.html.*

Black, D. Grant, with files from Barb Righton. "How a Small Prairie Town Got a Breath of New Life." *Canadian Living* online. *www.canadianliving.com/life/community/how-a-small-prairie-town-got-a-breath-of-new-life.*

Bohi, Charles W., and H. Roger Grant. "The Country Railroad Station of Manitoba." *Manitoba Pageant 23,* no. 3. *www.mhs.mb.ca/docs/pageant/23/railroadstation. shtml.*

"Brandon CPR Depot's New Lease on Life." *West End Dumplings* (blog). *http://westenddumplings.blogspot. ca/2011/03/brandon-cpr-stations-new-lease-on-life. html.*

"Canada's Historic Places: A Federal, Provincial and Territorial Collaboration." *www.historicplaces.ca/.*

Canadian Northern Society. "Big Valley, Alberta." *www. canadiannorthern.ca/BigValley.*

Canadian Northern Society. "Camrose, Alberta." *www. canadiannorthern.ca/Camrose.*

Canadian Northern Society. "Meeting Creek, Alberta." *www.canadiannorthern.ca/MeetingCreek.*

"Canadian Pacific Railway Heritage Park and Interpretive Centre." *www.cprstationportage.ca.*

CAW/TCA Canada, National Council 4000. "CN vacates downtown Edmonton's landmark CN Tower." *www. cawcouncil4000.com/08may12_cn_vacates_edmonton_ cntower.html.*

CBC News, Saskatchewan. "Historic Moose Jaw Hotel Another Step Closer to Demolition." *http://www. cbc.ca/news/canada/saskatchewan/story/2009/03/11/ brunswick-hotel.html.*

Champ, Joan. "Bienfait Hotel: Mute Witness to Troubled Times." *Railway & Main Saskatchewan Small-Town Hotels* (blog). *http://hotelhistories.blogspot. ca/2011/05/bienfait-hotel-mute-witness-to-troubled. html.*

"Celebrate Old Strathcona." *http://oldstrathcona.ca/about.*

City of Edmonton Historic Resource Management Program. "High Level Bridge."

www.edmonton.ca/city_government/documents/InfraPlan/ HighLevelBridge.pdf.

City of Edmonton Heritage Management Resource Program. "MacDonald Hotel, 10065-100 Street." www.edmonton.ca/city_government/documents/ InfraPlan/MacdonaldHotel.pdf.

City of Saskatoon. "CPR Station." www.sasktoon.ca.

"Coutts Train Station: Architectural Rehabilitation." www.rkharchitecture.com/rkh_041210_015.htm.

"CPR and Brandon Through the Years." Collated from the Hillman Brandon Archive Series. www.hillmanweb. com/brandon/cpr.html.

"Designated Grain Elevators in Alberta." www.grainel evatorsalberta.ca.

Dunnottar Station Museum. "Remembering the Role of the CPR Beach Trains." http://dunnottarstation.org/ museum.

"East Central Alberta Country Cruisin', Trains and Trestles." www.braedalberta.ca.

East Central Alberta Heritage Society. "Preserving our rail heritage." www.albertarailheritage.com.

Edmonton Radial Railway Society. "High Level Bridge," "High Level Bridge Streetcar," and "Fort Edmonton Park." www.edmonton-radial-railway.ab.ca.

"Exploring Warren's Historic Grain Elevator." www.west interlaketradingcompany.com.

The Fairmont Hotel Macdonald. "Hotel history." www. fairmont.com/EN_FA/property/MAC/AboutUs/ hotelhistory.htm.

"Five Prairie Giants: The Inglis Elevator Row National Historic Site." www.ingliselevators.com.

Footloose Caboose Lodge. "Humble Beginnings." www. footloosecaboose.com/beginnings.htm.

"The Forks Historic Rail Bridge." www.theforks.com/ attractions/at-the-forks/the-forks-historic-rail-bridge.

"The Forks History." www.theforks.com/about/history.

Forth Junction Project. "Railway Stations of Central Alberta." www.forthjunction.com/rail-stations.htm.

Government of Alberta, Cultural and Community Services. "Brooks Aqueduct: National and Provincial Historic Site." www.history.alberta.ca/brooksaqueduct.

Government of Manitoba, Historic Resources Branch. "Explore our Heritage: Provincial Heritage Sites by Name." www.gov.mb.ca/chc/hrb/prov/index.html.

_____. "Explore Our Heritage: Municipal Heritage Sites." www.gov.mb.ca/chc/hrb/mun/index.html.

Gravelbourg District Museum. "Heritage Walking Tour: A Walk Through History." www.gravelbourg.ca/ html/e/visitors/heritagewalkingtour.html.

Great Western Railway Ltd. "A Shortline Railway Serving Southwestern Saskatchewan." www.greatwesternrail. com.

"The Greater Winnipeg Water District Railway." www. winnipeg.ca/waterandwaste/dept/railway.stm.

"Heritage Character Statement, FHBRO, Number 99-142, Churchill Manotoba VIA Rail/CNR Station." www. historicplaces.ca.

Herrington, Ross. "Statement of Heritage Significance: Canadian Northern Railway Bridge Prince Albert." *www.tpcs.gov.sk.ca/PABridge.*

_____."Statement of Heritage Significance: Skytrail (Canadian Pacific Railway) Bridge, Town of Outlook." *www.tpcs.gov.sk.ca/OutlookBridge.*

_____."Statement of Heritage Significance: The Crooked Bridge, Town of Nipawin." *www.tpcs.gov.sk.ca/NipawinBridge.*

_____."Statement of Heritage Significance: The St. Louis (Grand Trunk Pacific Railway) Bridge, St. Louis." *www.tpcs.gov.sk.ca/StLouisBridge.*

"Historic Rowley: An Amazing Ghost Town With an Undying Spirit." *www.starlandcounty.com/rowley.htm.*

Historic Sites and Monuments Board of Canada. "Directory of Designated Heritage Railway Stations." *www.pc.gc.ca/eng/clmhc-hsmbc/heritage/listegares-liststations.aspx.*

"History of the Railroad in Hanna Alberta." *http://www.hanna.ca/Home/Roundhouse/RailHistory.aspx.*

Manitoba Agricultural Museum. *http://ag-museum.mb.ca.*

The Manitoba Historical Society. "Historic Sites of Manitoba." *www.mhs.mb.ca/docs/sites/index.shtml.*

_____. "Northern Prairie Steamboats." *www.mhs.mb.ca/docs/steamboats/index.html.*

McGuire, Don. "The Railway History of Wainwright." Wainwright Railway Preservation Society. *www.rail-park.org/stories/index.html.*

"Melville CN Station Restoration Project." *www.melvilleadvance.com/CN_Station_Restoration/CN_Station_Restoration.html.*

Mullin, L.T. "Moon," Eldon Owens, and Dick Meacher. eds. Erin Loch and Paul Johnson. "Together at last." Sukanen Ship Pioneer Village Museum. *www.sukanenmuseum.ca.*

"Nanton Heritage Railway." *www.nantonelevators.com.*

"New Improved Heritage Park, 2009 (Calgary)." Canadian Railway News. *www.OKthePK.ca.*

"Northern Alberta Railways Company, 1929–1980." *www.peaceriverchamber.com/history_of_peace_river.html.*

University of Alberta Libraries. "Peel's Prairie Province." *http://peel.library.ualberta.ca/index.html.*

Pettypiece, Paul. "Railway Heritage Preservation in Central Alberta." *www.paulpettypiece.com/rail_heritage_preservation.htm.*

_____. "The Calgary and Edmonton Railway." *www.paulpettypiece.com/c_and_e_railway.htm.*

"Prairie Dog Central Railway." *www.pdcrailway.com.*

Railroad Historical Society Inc. "Extant Railroad/Railway Structures in Manitoba, Saskatchewan, Alberta." *www.rrhs.org.*

"Railway trestle… 1919 wooden railway trestle." *www.waskatenau.ca/trestle.htm.*

The Saskatchewan Railway Museum. *www.saskrailmuseum.org.*

"Second Avenue, History." *www.secondavenuesaskatoon.com.*

Siamandas, George. "Transcona, Winnipeg's Railway Town." *http://timemachine.siamandas.com/PAGES/more%20 stories/TRANSCONA.htm.*

Siamandas, George. "Winnipeg's Union Station." *http:// timemachine.siamandas.com/PAGES/winnipeg_ stories/CNSTATION.htm.*

"Significant Dates in Canadian Railway History." Colin Churcher's Railway Pages. *www.railways.incanada. net/candate/candate.htm.*

"Surviving Steam Locomotives in Canada." *www.steam locomotive.com/lists/?country=CAN.*

Thunder Rail Ltd. *www.arborfieldsk.ca/thunder_rail. htm.*

Town of Bassano. "Bassano Dam." *www.bassano.ca/ BassanoDam.php.*

Town of Ogema. "The Ogema Train Project: Tracking Time in the New Millenium." *www.ogema.ca/ogema-train-station-project.html.*

Town of Outlook. "Skytrail, Canada's Longest Pedestrian Bridge." *http://town.outlook.sk.ca/skytrail.*

"Tunnels of Moose Jaw: Visiting the Tunnels." *www.tunnels ofmoosejaw.com.*

Wainwright Railway Preservation Society. "Wainwright Rail Park." *www.railpark.org.*

"Water Tower — Kenaston Saskatchewan." *www.kenaston. ca.*

"Who Saved the Royal Alexandra Café: The Story of Allan and Donni Stern." *www.crowsnest.bc.ca/alexandra/ sterns01.html.*

Vanterpool, Alan. "A Brief History of Alberta's Railways." Alberta Railway Museum. *www.albertarailway museum.com/a-brief-history-of-albertas-railways. html.*

Winnipeg Railway Museum. "The Countess of Dufferin." *www.wpgrailwaymuseum.com/loco-countess.html.*

Wilson, D.M. "Monarch Alberta: History." The Virtual Crowsnest Highway. *www.crowsnest-highway.ca/ cgi-bin/citypage.pl?city=MONARCH.*

Yanko, Dave. "Luck and Legacy (Regina Casino)." *www. virtualsk.com/current_issue/luck.html.*

_____. "The St. Louis Ghost Train." *www.virtualsk.com/ current_issue/ghost_train.html.*

Index

All page entries in italics indicate that the subject is in an image.

Also by Ron Brown

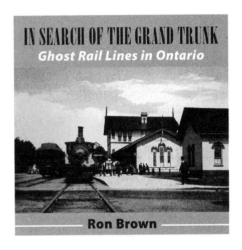

In Search of the Grand Trunk
Ghost Rail Lines in Ontario
978-1554888825
$24.99

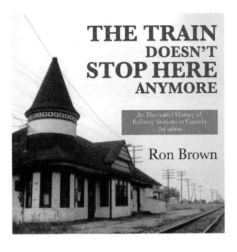

The Train Doesn't Stop Here Anymore
An Illustrated History of Railway Stations in Canada
978-1550027945
$29.99

Explore Ontario's forgotten rail lines and experience the legacy and lore of this the vital railway era of Ontario's history. At its peak between 1880 and the 1920s, Ontario was criss-crossed by more than 20,000 kilometres of rail trackage. Today, only a fraction remains. These are but a distant memory as most of Ontario's once essential transportation links lie abandoned and largely forgotten. But perhaps not entirely — many rights of way have become rail trails, and now witness hikers, cyclists, equestrians, and snowmobilers. Others, sadly, are overgrown and barely visible. Yet, regardless of how one follows these early routes, one will find preserved stations, historic bridges, and railway-era buildings, all of which recall this bygone era.

Despite the "green" benefits of rail travel, Canada has lost much of its railway heritage. Across the country, stations have been bulldozed and rails ripped up. Once the heart of communities large and small, stations and tracks have left little more than a gaping hole in Canada's landscapes. This book revisits the times when railways were the country's economic lifeline, and the station the social centre. Although most have vanished, the book celebrates the survival of that heritage in stations that have been saved or remain in use. The book will appeal to anyone who has links with our rail era, or who simply appreciates the value of Canada's built heritage.

Available at your favourite bookseller.

What did you think of this book?
Visit *www.dundurn.com* for reviews, videos, updates, and more!